M000012115

Praise for *Dare to Answer*

"Like a wise conversation that lasts deep into the night, John Busacker inspires all of us seeking to live a meaningful life."

Richard Leider, International Best-selling Author of
The Power of Purpose, Repacking Your Bags, and *Life Reimagined*

"What may be true about me today is not the complete Truth about how God sees me or what He calls me to be. I am a work in progress. Here, John Busacker dares to remind us of key questions, which Jesus asked for the purpose of drawing us into the Truth designed for our lives. Will we *Dare to Answer*?"

Jay Bennett, Chairman, National Christian Foundation

"John Busacker has the very rare skill of being able to make the Word come alive in a refreshing and poignant way by relating the life and teachings of Jesus through fascinating contemporary stories and observations. He weaves both humor and heartbreak into a wonderful mosaic in *Dare to Answer*."

Ward Brehm, Former Chairman, United States
Africa Development Foundation and Twin Cities Humanitarian

"So often Christians have thought it is our job to defend the truth through well-thought-through biblical arguments. John's thoughtful writings have offered a new paradigm that allows for questions and not answers to be the primary posture of a Christian. John's insight around eight of Jesus' questions has had a significant impact on how I go about engaging in conversations with the spiritual seekers in our community."

Kurt Vickman, Founder, Good Grocer

"The kind of wisdom and insight John Busacker reveals in this book was not come to by settling for easy answers but by asking really hard questions—mostly of himself. They're the kind of questions that, if you stay with them, will drive you down deep into your motives, and your heart and to where you really live and to what you really love. I highly recommend John's book, but get ready to dig down deep."

David Johnson, Senior Pastor, Church of the Open Door

DARE TO
ANSWER

Copyright © 2015 by Worthy Inspired, a division of Worthy Media, Inc.

ISBN 978-1-61795-475-7

Published by Worthy Inspired, an imprint of Worthy Publishing Group, a division of
Worthy Media, Inc.
134 Franklin Road, Suite 200, Brentwood, Tennessee 37027.

Unless indicated otherwise, Scripture is taken from The Message. Copyright © 1993, 1994,
1995, 1996, 2000, 2001, 2002. Used by permission of NavPress Publishing Group.

Scripture verses marked NIV are from THE HOLY BIBLE, NEW INTERNATIONAL
VERSION®, NIV® Copyright © 1973, 1978, 1984, 2011 by Biblica, Inc.® Used by permission.
All rights reserved worldwide.

All rights reserved. No part of this publication may be reproduced, stored in a retrieval
system, or transmitted in any form or by any means—electronic, mechanical, photocopy,
recording, scanning, or other—except for brief quotations in critical reviews or articles,
without the prior written permission of the publisher.

Cover Design by Kim Russell / Wahoo Designs
Page Layout by Bart Dawson

Printed in the United States of America

1 2 3 4 5—LBM—19 18 17 16 15

DARE TO ANSWER

8 Questions That Awaken Your Faith

JOHN BUSACKER

WORTHY®
Inspired

To Elvin Monroe "Monty" Sholund
my dear mentor:
His penetrating questions awakened my faith.
His persistent encouragement
instilled God's calling.

CONTENTS

INTRODUCTION
An Invitation to Answer

Life is filled with questions. Some we ask, but often the really important ones are those we dare to answer.

- How does God want to use me?
- Who am I—really?
- What really matters?
- What do I believe?

Once we have dared to answer the important questions, things that are repetitious, casual, surface, trivial, or simplistic no longer satisfy. We hunger for so much more.

We are designed to go deep with God—by God Himself.

Paul describes God's desire for us to go deeper as our destiny—our best life. He tells his friends:

God's wisdom is something mysterious that goes deep into the interior of his purposes. You don't find it lying around on the surface. It's not the latest message, but more like the oldest—what God determined as the way to bring out his best in us, long before we ever arrived on the scene (1 Corinthians 2:7).

But how do we do that? He can seem way out of our league, inaccessible, out of our grasp. And the truth is—He is! This is how David describes the enormous chasm between God and us:

God's love is meteoric, his loyalty astronomic, / His purpose titanic, his verdicts oceanic (Psalm 36:5–6).

How do you connect with love so vast, purpose so immense, wisdom so deep?

Clearly, God has asked us to draw near to Him to narrow the gap. And, when we do, there's hope for you and for me. David goes on to describe this hope when he says:

Yet in his largeness nothing gets lost; / Not a man, not a mouse, slips through the cracks (Psalm 36:6).

The God who cares about the location of every sparrow on the planet and has the very hairs on our head numbered is interested in every detail of our life. He will talk to us about the news, weather, and sports. But He wants more from us *and for us*. He wants to bridge the chasm by going beyond idle chatter and simplistic answers. God invites us to go deeper with Him.

The good news is God invites us and then He takes the initiative in leading us to where deep in our heart we most want to go. How?

He takes us deeper and draws us closer with questions—tough questions, personal questions, searching questions, transforming questions, deep questions.

God doesn't want us to be merely *interested* in Him. He wants us to be *intimate* with Him. He yearns to deepen our faith—from feeble to fierce, from predictable to passionate.

By answering His questions for ourselves, we begin to discover the true object of our desire, the source of our fear, the uniqueness of our identity, the focus of our compassion, the real measure of our wealth, and the only lasting love of our life. We begin to really know God. And to know Him is to love Him!

Are you willing to risk living in God's questions? The adventure will undoubtedly cause you to experience uncertainty and restlessness. But the result of leaning into God's questions is the exhilaration of a deep faith that is untamed in its expression and unimaginable in its outcome. It is worth the wild ride!

But God is God. I'm not sure I've ever heard Him ask me any questions.

Let me assure you, God's questions are right in front of you. I discovered them while reading through the Gospels. In one of those aha moments of life, I realized that when Jesus posed simple but poignant questions to those He encountered, He was asking the very same questions of . . . me . . . of you.

What a humbling and gratifying breakthrough for me. The God of all things, in the Person of Jesus Christ, was bridging the chasm between us. He was inviting me to go deeper.

I humbly echo the same invitation to you. I know you want to go deeper in your faith. I can't tell you what that will look like. I'm still on my own journey of daring to answer. Your journey is between you and God. But I know that when you answer eight questions Jesus poses to you, you will find God's destiny for you.

The starting point for our journey is the simple, yet profoundly challenging question of our desire, *"What do you want?"* The answer—the real answer, the deep answer—is the pivotal question of our devotion, *"Do you truly love Me?"*

REFLECT AND RESPOND

To enrich your spiritual adventure, I want to encourage you to complete the Reflect and Respond activities found at the conclusion of each chapter. If you are like me, you might find the experience even more enriching when explored with others. Like the questions Jesus poses to you, you will find the activities both simple and profound when you reach higher and go deeper than trite, practiced, responses.

You will be challenged to:

- **READ** additional Scripture to expand your understanding of each question.
- **REFLECT** on questions to stimulate discovery individually or in a small group dialogue.
- **RESPOND** to a challenge to boldly practice each of Jesus' questions.

Let's get started on going deeper with God together!

*The next day John was there again with two
of his disciples. When he saw Jesus passing by, he said,
"Look, the Lamb of God!" When the two disciples heard
him say this, they followed Jesus. Turning around,
Jesus saw them following and asked, "What do you want?"*

—

John 1:35–38, NIV

Chapter One

WHAT DO YOU WANT?

A QUESTION OF DESIRE

It's a close game. In the final few minutes, the underdog pulls off the upset. If you were cheering for the underdog, you are delirious with joy. If your team was favored to win but mysteriously didn't "show up," you are inconsolable. Now you have to listen to postgame analysis and relive your joy or misery.

The sports commentator tries to explain why a team that shouldn't have won beat a team that should have won and invariably uses a trite phrase about the victor: "they wanted it more."

There are a lot of things I want in life. I think it would be terrific to run a sub-three-hour marathon, for example. However, I haven't and I likely won't. I sort of want to, but it's not my passion; it's not my true heart's desire.

This is a book about going deeper in your spiritual walk. The fact that you have picked up *Dare to Answer* makes me suspect you have already seen Jesus "passing by" in your life. Maybe someone said to you, "Look! There He is. He's the One. He makes all the difference in the world." And you started following . . . maybe at a distance . . . maybe a little reluctantly.

But now He's turned to you. He's looked you in the eyes. He's asked, "What do you want?"

What do you want? The beauty and power of that question is it is relevant whether you've known Jesus your entire life or just a few short months or don't know Him at all yet.

As you read on, you will discover that this is no easy question to answer, no matter where you are on your journey. A superficial answer is as dangerous as no answer at all. It is not for the faint of heart. You are going to have to truly "want it" to know it.

That's a big part of what it means to dare to answer.

Scaling Mount Kilimanjaro

I was immediately drawn to Elias. A short, powerfully built man with a radiant smile, Elias (Swahili for Elijah) had stopped counting his successful Kilimanjaro summit attempts when he had reached 200. At age thirty, he already embodied the quiet wisdom of experience and clear passion of calling that inspired confident followership. After meeting him, I decided pretty quickly that if I was going to attempt the summit of Kilimanjaro, I wanted Elias to be my guide.

My eleven fellow climbers and I gathered around in a tight circle as Elias kneeled over a dog-eared map of the mountain. He described the route through five eco-systems we would be taking in our ascent and descent of Kilimanjaro. We would begin hiking through the Montane forest, camp the fourth evening in the Reusch crater bracketed by the seventy-five-foot ice wall of the Fortwangler Glacier, climb to the summit early the next morning, then descend along the Mweka route. All told, the journey would take six days.

Elias pointed out landmarks on the topographic map and described both the physical and emotional obstacles we would encounter during the climb. As he spoke, we were all feeling the giddy anticipation of success, the quiet fear

of possible failure, and a chafing restlessness to begin—
the powerful mixture that precedes most great adventures
in life.

After less than fifteen minutes, Elias ended his narrative,
slowly turned to look at each of us as if he was looking directly in our hearts and asked, "What do you want?"

Great question! What *did* we want? What did I want?

A sense of achievement? A story to tell my grandchildren some day? A beautiful trek through God's glorious creation? Did I want to test myself—and make sure as a middle-
aged man I still "had it"? All the above? Something more or
different?

Like Jesus, Elias posed a simple but poignant question
that goes straight to the heart and, when honestly confronted
and answered, brings so much clarity and purpose to life.

Elias was laid back but sharp as a tack. This wasn't just
a casual ice-breaker question for him. He wanted to know
what was driving us. He was giving us an opportunity to
know ourselves a little better.

Throughout the next six days, he used our answers to
build relationships certainly, but he also used our answers—
our own words, our own stated desires—to encourage and
challenge each of us in unique ways.

I told you Elias had a quiet wisdom. He was a great

leader. I truly believe his amazing ability to effectively lead us was in direct proportion to the way he helped us clarify our own desires for climbing Mount Kilimanjaro.

Have you ever taken the time to clarify your own desires? Have you ever searched for the deepest desire of your heart and life?

Jesus' First Question

It is no accident that Jesus asked such a personal life-clarifying question early in His ministry. It is the first crucial question He used to ignite followership in twelve men who would change the world forever with the power of His teaching and His work and presence in their lives. It is the essential question He asks of us today to continue His world-changing work. He shows up in our life, sometimes unexpectedly, to ask through both subtle stirrings and traumatic life events, "What do you want?"

Like His Father, Jesus is all-knowing and all-powerful, but as with the other questions in this book, He will not answer for us. We must weigh in for ourselves. Clarifying what we truly desire is the departure point on our journey to depth.

The two men of whom Jesus asked the original question were followers of John the Baptist. There was a wildness, an unrestrained boldness about John that attracted these men and many others to the wilderness. When Eugene Peterson describes John in *The Message* translation of the Bible, he uses vivid phrases that capture John's person. The one that stands out to me most forcefully is, "I'm thunder in the desert" (John 1:23).

John the Baptist himself had a clear passion of calling and purpose. He had answered in his own life the question of what he really wanted. He had discovered the God-given desire of his life. It made him bold. Fearless. It enabled him to ignite the energy, expectation, and imagination of a whole generation of people weary of Roman oppression and a worn-out religion of rules. When Jesus showed up on the scene, John proved true to his calling. He didn't try to hold onto his popularity. He knew who he was and what he wanted. He pointed Jesus out for all of his followers to see: "Look, the Lamb of God!"

A few of his followers got jealous when their comrades left to follow Jesus. Not John. He may have been wild at heart, but he understood his purpose. He simply said:

"A person can receive only what is given them from heaven. You yourselves can testify that I said, 'I am not the Messiah but am sent ahead of him.' The bride belongs to the bridegroom. The friend who attends the

bridegroom waits and listens for him, and is full of joy when he hears the bridegroom's voice. That joy is mine, and it is now complete. He must become greater; I must become less" (John 3:27-30, NIV).

Wouldn't it be wonderful to know who you are and what you are called to do as clearly as John? What if I told you that was possible?

With just one word and two days experience these two disciples of John abruptly turned and began to trail after and then run after Jesus. Others soon followed. Had John not already personally answered God's question, "What do you want?" such a sudden change of allegiance would have led to chaos and conflict.

There must have been something missing from the two disciples' lives, a spiritual discontent deep within their heart. They sensed and, with John's help, *knew* that only this carpenter from Nazareth could satisfy what they truly wanted. Despite being avid followers of John, they dropped everything and turned on a dime to pursue a different leader. They were *seekers*. Os Guinness describes what I believe was in their heart:

They were looking for something. They were people to whom life, or a part of life, had suddenly become a point of wonder, a question, a problem, or a crisis. This happened so intensely that they were stirred to look for an answer beyond their present answers and to clarify their position in life.

Jesus' very presence was posing a new question that needed a new answer. The followers of John became seekers of Jesus.

That's what happens when we truly see Jesus. We see something—*Someone*—new, and only a new, deeper answer to what we really want will suffice.

I want to repeat for emphasis and to hold up as a role model for the process of answering this question, aren't you glad John had already experienced the wonder of recognizing the "Lamb of God" and encouraging his followers to continue their quest?

What About You?

Are you a seeker also? Do you have a sense that something deep inside is missing? Has life become a point of wonder, a question, a problem, or a crisis for you? Is there a restlessness that is unstilled by work, school, friendship, money, church, or even family? Do you feel as if you are treading water, making no progress? If so, perhaps God is asking you the same question today—"What do you want?"—with the intent to engage you in a new, world-changing work. So what do you *really* want?

But before you make a mad headlong dash to answer that question with a quick answer, stop, slow down, and wait. All of us have come up with quick responses on what we want only to discover ourselves going in the completely wrong direction.

Waiting for *Desire* to Happen

We want to maintain at least the illusion that we have it all figured out and are in control of our life, work, relationships, and even religion—that we are always moving steadily forward. But then God poses a new question in our heart, which brings an unsettledness, a stirring in our soul that invites us to again become a seeker. We are awakened by a new inquiry in our soul and consumed by finding a new answer. We hunger for the answers.

Author Brennan Manning, who learned through the depths of alcoholism that control is an illusion, encourages us to pray:

I surrender my will and my life to you today, without reservation and with humble confidence for you are my loving Father. Set me free from self-consciousness, from anxiety about yesterday and tomorrow and from the tyranny of the approval and disapproval of others, that I may find joy and delight simply and solely in pleasing you. Let your plan for my life and the lives of all your children gracefully unfold one day at a time.

I regularly charge off after my own desires before checking in on God's direction. It is said that human beings are the only creatures on the planet who speed up when lost or confused. We are impatient. We don't take time to discover what we truly want. We settle for convenient, superficial, prepackaged answers.

David sums up God's perspective on speedy answers, on chasing after the first thing that comes to mind, when he declares: "I pray to God—my life a prayer—and *wait* for what he'll say and do" (Psalm 130:5).

Paradoxically, the initial path of seeking is to wait. David had discovered two critical truths about godly waiting. First, he is not shooting up a prayer at the last minute in hopes of getting some personal request granted. His *life* was a prayer. Much of the Psalms are David's prayer journal with God. He was in constant, intimate, brutally honest conversation with the Almighty. No wonder God Himself said of David: "I've searched the land and found this David, son of Jesse. He's a man whose heart beats to my heart, a man who will do what I tell him" (Acts 13:22).

Second, David was not waiting for God to catch up to his plan. We never express our heart's true desire by charging on ahead of God. We need to pause and pray. An African expression for patience is "waiting for time to happen." We must wait for God's desire to happen, in our heart.

What we are ultimately waiting for is the wisdom to discern God's will at each critical transition in our lives. This wisdom does not typically flow into a noisy, crowded mind. It seeps into a heart quieted by prayer. God's desire is a matter of the heart, not just the head. The word *desire* is most often coupled in the Bible with heart or heart's desire. Erwin McManus writes, "What can settle your mind will not settle your soul. It will stir it up." The desire of the heart is a much more powerful tug than that of the head.

My friend John, a Carmelite monk whose life is devoted to discerning matters of the heart through constant prayer, sent me this thought several years ago:

The inner life of prayer can best flourish in an atmosphere of silence, free from agitation and noise. In silent prayer we come face to face with ourselves and learn to reconcile the contradictions of our lives; the fears, anxieties and frustrations that lead to discouragement and illness. Something more begins to happen, mysteriously, in moments of deep serenity; we discover at the root of our being, the presence of the One who created us and calls us in love, and we emerge from this experience transformed by the quiet joy and gentle peace which radiates from the inner recesses of the heart.

The Heart of Desire

God approached David's son, Solomon, with the same question of desire: "Ask for whatever you want me to give you" (2 Chronicles 1:7, NIV). In other words, *what do you want*, Solomon?

There was no salary cap on these contract negotiations, no limitations on what Solomon could ask for or on what God could grant. Signing bonus? No problem. Guaranteed contract? Money? Fame? Power? Done. But what Solomon asked for was simply wisdom, "a discerning heart to govern [God's] people and to distinguish between right and wrong" (1 Kings 3:9, NIV).

God's answer back to Solomon?

Since this is your heart's desire and you have not asked for wealth, riches or honor, nor for the death of your enemies, and since you have not asked for a long life but for wisdom and knowledge to govern my people over whom I have made you king, therefore wisdom and knowledge will be given you. And I will also give you wealth, riches and honor, such as no king who was before you ever had and none after you will have (2 Chronicles 1:11-12, NIV).

I hesitate to think what I would ask for given the open checkbook of heaven! And yet God's hand is open to give us our heart's desire *if* (and this is the critical *if)* our heart's desire is aligned with God's desire. How do we know if they are one and the same? How do we discern if the longings of our heart are God-inspired?

As I said at the beginning of the chapter, I want to run a fast marathon. But it isn't my heart's true desire. I believe the answer of true desire can only be discovered when we align what we want with what God wants for us.

That sounds simple. Why is it so hard?

Blinded by the White

Webster's New World dictionary defines *orientation* as "the homing faculty of certain animals." We are all born with a spiritual homing faculty. Instinctively, we know if we are on or off course. St. Augustine wrote, "You have made us for Yourself, and our hearts are restless until they find their rest in You." Restlessness is our God-given homing faculty. Try as we may with work, recreation, food, sex, family, money, religion, or whatever else, we feel lost and so disoriented when we go our own way without a thought of God.

The advertising industry in the U.S. spends billions of dollars annually trying to jam God's homing beacon. They bombard us through pop-ups, e-mail, TV, radio, newspapers, magazines, billboards, and social media with more than 3,000 ads per day. Through brilliantly crafted messages, their job is to create desire. You will be happy, successful, attractive, powerful, safe, and fulfilled if:

- You drive this.
- Smell like that.
- Dress like this.
- Have that smartphone.
- Live in this neighborhood.
- Invest in that fund.

The list of what we really *want* and think we *need* goes on and on. Have you ever wondered why we really don't feel any different after we get this or that?

In a word, the role of advertisers is to *dis-orient* us, to cause us to live on the surface rather than plumb the depths of our true desires. But to become disoriented is to risk becoming totally lost.

I was climbing at Mount Rainier National Park on a late spring day with my older son, Brett. We had gotten off to a late start but were still hoping to climb from the parking lot of Paradise (aptly named) to the ranger hut at Camp Muir, an ascent of about 5,000 feet. The weather was deteriorating with intermittent periods of sun, snow, clouds, rain, and gusty winds. At about the halfway point, two climbers descending from the summit met us. They cautioned us that the conditions at Camp Muir were "downright nasty" and suggested we turn around soon. Heeding their advice, Brett and I decided to hike just a hundred feet farther, snap a quick picture of a breathtaking vista, and begin our descent back to the car.

No sooner had we turned around, when we were suddenly enveloped by a complete whiteout, a dense cloud that swallowed us up, immediately eliminating any sense of direction or depth perception. Our eyes filled with dancing white spots as our brains tried to register our distance to any discernable mountain feature. We were both totally disoriented. Although we were off the glacier and in no danger of falling into a crevasse, I had a dull fear that we might still stray off our path and spend a long day and possibly evening wandering in circles. Our saving grace that afternoon was a series of brightly colored wands planted every ten to twenty yards in the snow by the U.S. Park Service, outlining the path to Paradise.

It is painfully easy to become disoriented in our journey through life, caught up in the whiteout of our own superficial desires—and the desires of others—and thus put ourselves in danger of wandering in circles on the path to Paradise. One minute it seems that we are navigating in the clear sunshine of God's calling and in the next we are lost in a deep cloudbank of our own causing. Our homing faculty tells us that we are off track, but we can't see to find our way out. Thankfully, God anticipated our tendency to become disoriented and has planted brightly colored wands to help us navigate our way home.

Transformed Desires

Paul cautioned the people of Rome to "not conform to the pattern of this world, but be transformed by the renewing of your mind. Then you will be able to test and approve what God's will is—his good, pleasing and perfect will" (Romans 12:1 NIV).

Wouldn't it be great to know God's good, pleasing, and

perfect will for our lives? Paul tells us we can. It begins with renewed minds. Our minds are renewed through open-hearted time in God's Word.

God's words are our brightly colored wands that keep us on the path to Paradise. If we are going to be able to discern between good and unhealthy or lesser desires, we need to regularly spend time in His book sharpening our mind. God's words are "living and active" (Hebrews 4:12, NIV), or as Eugene Peterson describes in *The Message*, "His powerful Word is sharp as a surgeon's scalpel, cutting through everything, whether doubt or defense, laying us open to listen and obey." If we are to cut through the dense cloudbank of marketing noise—a siren call to conform, to just fit in—in order to discern God's desire, we must follow the wands of His words. God's desires always line up with His words. He is perfectly consistent.

This is no magical formula. Even if we listen to our heart and read the Word consistently, we can still find ourselves a long way off course. History is riddled with examples of horrific and sometimes just plain stupid acts that have been committed in the name of God's will. Scripture is the narrative of God's great love for us. Wisely and humbly used, it lovingly displays God's desires through our actions. When employed recklessly, with arrogance and self-interest, it can have the opposite effect. The Word does not indiscriminately endorse our point of view or merely prove our position over others.

We must, therefore, triangulate our heart's desires and our own understanding of God's Word with the counsel of other Jesus-following friends who evidence God's wisdom in their own walk. The Bible is full of encouragement to seek the counsel of others willing to love us and speak truth to action in our life and plans.

- "The way of a fool seems right to him, but a wise man listens to advice" (Proverbs 12:15, NIV).
- "Plans fail for lack of counsel, but with many advisers they succeed" (Proverbs 15:22, NIV).
- "As iron sharpens iron, so one person sharpens another" (Proverbs 27:17, NIV).

Without the wisdom and encouragement of others, we are prone to pursue selfish desires, fun desires, or even "pretty good" desires rather than God's desires. The enemy of great is what is merely good. There is nothing inherently wrong with pretty good desires, except when they keep us from pursuing God's great desires for our lives.

God's great desires are ultimately the deepest desires of our heart. He put them there.

His Desire for Us

In a painful, sobering, and eye-opening observation at a REVEAL conference at the Willow Creek Church in suburban Chicago, Bill Hybels proposed that the largest gap between faith and practice exists not between seekers and believers but between immature followers and Jesus-centered followers. The less mature believe that God is automatically for their plans and agenda—whatever those plans and that agenda might be. Jesus followers have given up their lives and plans in complete surrender to Him. It is no longer about them.

May I gently suggest to you that your true desire will never be found by focusing solely on yourself? It really isn't about you or me, even at the point of what we superficially perceive to be what we really want.

This is the great and deliberate contradiction in Jesus' first question. Even though He asks what we want, He is not for *our* plans, some of which will lead us on paths we should never take. He is for *His* plans, planted in our heart, supported by His Word, and confirmed by other Jesus followers. The essence of His question is ultimately not about *our* desire; it is about discovering *His* desire for us and in us. In the end, what will truly quench the burning thirst in our spirit and deepen our faith is a relentless pursuit of His desire.

Nothing else will satisfy. The insatiable nature of our own pursuits bears this out.

How's That Working for You?

When our two sons were teenagers and we saw them charging down a path that we sensed would not have a positive outcome, we tried to sneak up on them with a powerful checking question: "How's that working for you?" This is a great question to assess the pursuit of our own desires as well. Our choices have consequences—and so do our desires.

Imagine being a contestant on a game show where you must choose between what is behind either Door #1 or Door #2. Let me list the items behind both doors:

Door #1

- repetitive, loveless, cheap sex
- a stinking accumulation of mental and emotional garbage
- frenzied and joyless grabs for happiness
- trinket gods
- magic-show religion
- paranoid loneliness
- cutthroat competition
- all-consuming-yet-never-satisfied wants

- a brutal temper
- impotence to love or be loved
- divided homes and divided lives
- small-minded and lopsided pursuits
- the vicious habit of depersonalizing everyone into a rival
- uncontrolled and uncontrollable addiction
- ugly parodies of community

Door #2

- affection for others
- exuberance about life
- serenity
- willingness to stick with things
- sense of compassion in the heart
- conviction that a basic holiness permeates things and people
- loyal commitments
- not needing to force our way in life
- able to marshal and direct our energies wisely

Which door would *you* choose? The rewards behind Door #1 or Door #2 are ours to receive as we decide daily which desires to pursue. The first door is a path of our own selfish desires, the second a path of God-inspired desires. Door #1 lives are marked by the restlessness of disorientation, always wanting more or different, but never having a sense of rest from striving or freedom from worry. Door #2 lives are marked by a deep joy and contentment because the desires pursued are perfectly in tune with God's heart.

Don't just take my word for it. You will find the outcomes listed above in Galatians 5:19-23.

As God continues to encounter us and ask, "What do you want?" we must wait and listen to our heart, weigh our desires against God's words, seek wise counsel from faithful others, and then regularly check the outcomes of our pursuits.

Buying Time

What do you want? This is God's crucial first question. We are not wired as human beings created in the image of God to merely replicate but to learn and grow, to adventure and explore. Our desires define our direction, and our ultimate desire defines our destination. What we pursue reflects who we are and determines what we will become.

It is like saying, "Show me who you hang with, and I'll show you who you'll become." The followers of John wanted to hang with Jesus, and ultimately became like Him.

John's two disciples' response when Jesus asked, "What do you want," was a startled, "Where are you staying?"

They were not sure how to respond to such a direct inquiry. Their initial safe answer was a benign question of their own. I suspect they were buying time. Why get to the heart of the matter if they could stick to the news, weather, and sports? John's disciples sensed danger in the depth of Jesus' question.

I, too, feel unsettled when God plants longings in my heart. There is the intuitive sense that if I respond positively to what He asks of me I will have to move from my comfort zone, and, in that moment, lurks the realization that another great adventure is about to begin. The feelings of giddy anticipation, quiet fear, and chafing restlessness return.

In *Wild at Heart*, John Eldredge writes:

Most men think they are simply here on earth to kill time—and it's killing them. But the truth is precisely the opposite. The secret longing of your heart, whether it's to build a boat and sail it, to write a symphony and play it, to plant a field and care for it—those are the things you were made to do. But it's going to take risk, and danger, and there's the catch. Are we willing to live with the level of risk God invites us to? Something inside us hesitates.

There is a time to wait. We don't want to run ahead of God's plans for us. But when clarity comes, it is time to move. Isn't it funny that we will take mad dashes when we don't know God's will, but then slow down, stall, and buy time when we know it? I think there's a reason for that. It can be found in the next question Jesus poses to His followers then and today. To move us deeper in our faith journey, He poses a question to get at the core of our inertia: "Why are you so afraid?"

REFLECT AND RESPOND

READ the following Scripture:

- 2 Chronicles 1:7-12
- Galatians 5:19-23 (Preferably in *The Message*)

REFLECT on the following questions:

1. Are you a *seeker*? What is currently stirring in your heart?

2. How do you determine if your desires are bad? Merely good? Godly?

3. Which of the items behind Door #1 or #2 (Galatians 5:19-23) most accurately capture the current outcomes of your pursuits?

RESPOND to the following challenges:

- Commit to spending time each of the next thirty days in God's Word—seeking His "wands" for your life. The Old Testament book of *Proverbs* would provide you with great daily wisdom, but choose any passage of Scripture to pursue.

- Commit to finding and engaging one other Jesus follower who will give you wise council, ask the tough questions, and hold your toes to the coals of your commitment to go deeper in your faith in the next thirty days.

That day when evening came, he said to his disciples,
"Let us go over to the other side." Leaving the crowd
behind, they took him along, just as he was,
in the boat. There were also other boats with him.
A furious squall came up, and the waves broke over
the boat, so it was nearly swamped. Jesus was in the stern,
sleeping on a cushion. The disciples woke him
and said to him, "Teacher, don't you care if we drown?"
He got up, rebuked the wind and said to the waves,
"Quiet! Be still!" Then the wind died down and it was
completely calm. He said to his disciples,
"Why are you so afraid? Do you still have no faith?"

—

Mark 4:35-40, NIV

Chapter Two

WHY ARE YOU SO AFRAID?

A QUESTION OF FEAR

One memorable commercial several years ago featured a woman swimming laps in a pool. Back and forth, back and forth. Suddenly she stopped, stood up, and removed her goggles with a quixotic look. The silent words that appeared on the TV screen were simply, "What if?" The implication was that as she was swimming her mind was pondering possibilities that culminated with a workout-stopping big idea. What if?

What If?

What if? What if we risk actually answering the questions that God places within us? What if we practice salmon faith and swim upstream against the torrential current of the world's values and teachings? So much of what Jesus taught was directly opposite of the prevailing wisdom of His day. His teaching is just as revolutionary in our day. What if we trust His radical direction today—even if it flies in the face of the prevailing wisdom? What if we risk refocusing our resources on the poor and the lost rather than our own comfort? What if we risk declaring cultural attitudes on success and fulfillment as inadequate—as wrong—by our own attitudes and actions? What if we really take God's desire for our life seriously?

Stefan, a wonderfully gifted musician and speaker at the Upper Room Community, posed just this question to the assembled gathering one Sunday night. He challenged people to listen carefully to their hearts and then pick one of Jesus' revolutionary teachings and faithfully, courageously practice it for just one month.

What if . . .

- when you suddenly remember a grudge a friend has against you—you "abandon your offering, . . . go . . . and make things right" (Matthew 5:23).

- you "don't say anything you don't mean. . . . You don't make your words true by embellishing them with religious lace. . . . [You just] say 'yes' and 'no'" (Matthew 5:37).

- when "someone takes unfair advantage of you, [you] use the occasion to practice the servant life" (Matthew 5:41).

- when you give a luncheon or dinner, "you invite those who cannot repay you" (Luke 14:12-14, NIV).

- when you pray, you "find a quiet, secluded place so you won't be tempted to role-play before God" (Matthew 6:6).

- you "give your entire attention to what God is doing right now, and don't get worked up about what may or may not happen tomorrow" (Matthew 6:33).

- you "give to the one who asks you" (Matthew 4:42, NIV).

I thought about that message a lot, particularly Jesus' statement on true generosity. Then I had my first "what-if" moment. I encountered a homeless man at the end of an exit ramp, holding a cup and a sign with scrawled letters that read: *Unemployed—Need Money To Feed My Family*. What was my courageous, faith-filled response? I turned the other way, fiddled with the radio, and pretended to answer a call on my cell phone, all the while praying the light would turn green faster. Why did I have to choose the exit ramp with a "no turn on red" sign?

What does God expect of us? Just this: "He's already made it plain how to live, what to do, what God is looking for in men and women. It's quite simple: Do what is fair and just to your neighbor, be compassionate and loyal in your love, and don't take yourself too seriously—take God seriously" (Micah 6:8).

Taking God seriously at His word and striking out in the direction of His heart-felt call is likely to cause, at a minimum, anxiety and, more likely, deep fear—the panic that accompanies being into life over our head and out of control.

Jesus' Untimely Question

It is in just such a moment of panic for His disciples when Jesus intervenes with His seemingly untimely question. Of course when you are in what appears to be a life or death struggle, doesn't fear seem to be a normal response? Doesn't it seem unrealistic for Jesus to ask, "Why are you so afraid?" in such a moment? But that is precisely and intentionally the moment He chooses to ask His followers why they were so afraid. He uses that dramatic moment to call their faith forward into a deeper level of courage and conviction.

He asks the same question of us today, maybe in the moment when we feel most justified in our fears. As we sense the restlessness of our heart to be bolder in the face of our challenges in relationships, work, and faith, He asks us to step out, to take a stand, to take Him at His word. It is a question He will not answer for us. He leaves it up to us to identify and face our fears.

It was at Jesus' invitation that the disciples found themselves in such a fix in the first place. Having just completed a full day of teaching, Jesus told his small band of followers to leave the crowd behind and set out on a lake-crossing, faith-deepening journey. During the night, a sudden storm blows up and threatens to sink their small boat. Quickly overcome with abject terror, the followers cry out to Jesus, who amazingly is deep asleep—either with the exhaustion that comes from giving oneself fully to others or with the peace that must accompany being the master of meteorology.

Jesus' question about His disciples' fear is designed to take their eyes off the furious squall that threatened to sink them and refocus them squarely back on His presence and power. In his devotional *My Utmost for His Highest,* Oswald

Chambers writes of Peter's short-lived walk on top of the waves:

We step right out with recognition of God in some things, then self-consideration enters our lives and down we go. If we are truly recognizing our Lord, we have no business being concerned about how and where He engineers our circumstances. The things surrounding us are real, but when we look at them we are immediately overwhelmed and even unable to recognize Jesus. Then comes His rebuke "Why did you doubt?" We must let our actual circumstances be what they may, but keep recognizing Jesus, maintaining complete reliance on Him."

What About You?

Have you obediently followed what you thought to be God's desire planted in your heart only to find the sea of your life stirred up by some sudden squall? There is a fascinating and instructive sequence in this story of how God works in our lives to face our fears. He gives us a command and follows it with a challenge of faith.

But why does He have to make it so hard? Why not easy? Wouldn't that be more encouraging?

I believe that in order for us to go deeper in our faith,

He knows we must be forced to relinquish our self-reliance and confront our fears. When faith is easy we are tempted to default to the way of the world, dominated by self-interest and superficiality.

In the first chapter of this book we learned that our heart's true desire can only be found in aligning ourselves with God's desire—the desire that God has placed in our hearts is for Himself. Solomon in his wisdom said, "He has also set eternity in the hearts of men" (Ecclesiastes 3:11, NIV).

God doesn't want us to mistake fleeting and shallow desires with eternal desires, so He immediately challenges us to risk it all in order that we sink down roots of faith. We won't go deeper until our heart and mind are anchored deeply in Him. Only then will we experience dreams and desires that will not wither *when* (not *if*) the blast furnace of life is turned up.

Are you going through a storm in life that has you terrified? What if that was a good thing? What if that was confirmation that God believes in you so much He is willing to let you face your fears on the jagged edge of life?

Going Deeper Is Exhilarating—and Dangerous

A consistent pattern emerges in Scripture when God is preparing to accomplish something great through His people.

He always calls them to risk—to step out so far in faith that whatever it is they are about to attempt could never be accomplished were He not in the center of their actions.

- Noah is called to build a boat, anticipating a storm at a time when the earth had never yet seen rain. (See Genesis 6.)

- Abraham is called to slaughter his only son after waiting for 100 years to be a father. (See Genesis 22.)

- Joshua is called to cross the Jordan River at the peak of flood season in order to take hold of the land God promised. (See Joshua 3.)

- Three men—Shadrach, Meshach, and Abednego—are called to step into a blast furnace in order to defy the order of an ungodly leader. (See Daniel 3.)

- The prostitute Rahab is called to hide two spies—at the risk of her life—sent by Joshua to explore Jericho, thereby earning an honorable mention in Jesus' genealogy in Matthew 1. (See Joshua 2.)

- Ananias is called to minister to the murderer Saul, a man who wants to kill him and people like him, delivering a sobering message of "the hard suffering that goes with the job" of being a Christ-follower. (See Acts 9.)

Hebrews 11 is called the honor roll of faith. It details the lives of men and women who risked everything to answer God's invitation to take Him at His word and His promises. The list is so long, that the author concludes in:

I could go on and on, but I've run out of time. There are so many more—Gideon, Barak, Samson, Jephthah, David, Samuel, the prophets. . . . Through acts of faith, they toppled kingdoms, made justice work, took the promises for themselves. They were protected from lions, fires and sword thrusts, turned disadvantage to advantage, won battles, routed alien armies. Women received their loved ones back from the dead (verses 32-35a).

Sounds good so far doesn't it? They were conquerors! But don't stop reading there. The story continues:

There were those who, under torture, refused to give in and go free, preferring something better: resurrection. Others braved abuse and whips, and, yes, chains and dungeons. We have stories of those who were stoned, sawed in two, murdered in cold blood; stories of vagrants wandering the earth in animal skins, homeless, friendless, powerless—the world didn't deserve them!— making their way as best they could on the cruel edges of the world (verses 35b-38).

Huh? What did we just read? They ended up homeless? Friendless? Powerless? Sawed in two? Can't we just navigate the safe center rather than the "cruel edges of the world"?

All of these men and women were living out the life of godly risk described by William Barclay when he wrote:

> *The very essence of life is in risking life and spending life, not in saving and hoarding it. True, it is the way of weariness, of exhaustion, of giving to the uttermost, but it is better any day to burn out than to rust out, for that is the way to true joy and the way to God.*

My friend, going deeper with God is dangerous!

Going to the Other Side

Jesus invites the disciples to push out from the shore and "go over to the other side." This would have been no great sweat if the disciples had hugged the shoreline all the way around to the other side of the lake. Even if a strong storm blew in and they were swamped in the shallows, the disciples could merely get out and walk safely to shore. But the "other side" to which Jesus was calling them required sailing out into the deep. There was no time for a leisurely sailing trip. Or to be safe. On the other side was a region inhabited by the poorest

Gentiles—people who lived in caves that provided both a shelter for the living and a burial spot for the dead. Jesus was challenging His followers to leave behind superficial service to the already saved in order to courageously cross over into a radical new life of living for the least, the lost, and the left out. In the crossing was great discomfort, fear, and even a panic-filled cry for rescue.

Count me as one who prefers safe and leisurely. But that's not how faith is deepened. The fear caused by risk—outrageous faith—provides a life-changing epiphany moment that sets the course of the deeper life. It is when we boldly risk that we receive the unmistakable affirmation of God's presence and favor on the lifelong journey of faith, and our relationship with Him.

Brennan Manning challenges us:

Search your heart for the Isaac in your life—name it—money, face, reputation, prestige, love of stuff—and then place it on the altar as an offering to the Lord, and you will know the meaning of Abrahamic trust.

What is your "other side"? Who is your Isaac? Only when God breaks through our carefully erected walls of false self-sufficiency and forces us to cry out in fear to Him are we ready to truly trust. God is not moved by our circumstances. He is, however, moved to action when we, like the disciples, cry out to Him.

Can We Just Go Back to Reading Books?

When we choose to risk life rather than to save or hoard it, when we step into the deep waters or begin to cross over to the other side, we can expect to encounter resistance.

Call it spiritual physics. Taking action for God is often met by an opposite, and even greater, reaction from Satan. When the disciples pushed out into the deep waters, a "furious squall came up."

It was not only the weather that was furious but also the forces of evil. While Jesus slept, evil was aroused. Benign Sunday-going-to-church faith meets with little opposition, spiritually or physically. Satan pays little attention to the compliant attendees of holy huddles. They represent only a minor risk to him. But to step out into the deep water of courageous faith is to stir up active resistance, often in areas or relationships that are closest to us.

My friend Tom was a faithful and wise participant in a small men's group I led every other Friday morning for over ten years. He has a diverse background as a pastor and successful business leader. His active curiosity and life shaped by raising three boys all combined to make him a wonderful and razor-sharp witted contributor to the bi-weekly dialogue. He is a gifted communicator. Little did he know how God was going to use that gift in communicating to our small group.

Recently we had discussed the growing desire that several members had expressed. They were feeling called to move beyond our comfortable rhythm of meeting, discussing a book, praying, and catching up on each other's lives. We had engaged in a service project the previous spring, helping landscape a cloister for Carmelite monks, but had largely remained inwardly focused on supporting each other as men, fathers, and business people. Now, because of the confluence of several life circumstances, a number of the guys were feeling divinely led to take a bolder step into our collective faith journey. They actually wanted to *do* something with their faith. They wanted to cross to the "other side."

We discussed several options, from feeding street people to building homes for the homeless to supporting the education needs of women in rural Africa. As the dialog picked up enthusiasm, several of the men slowed things down and voiced the real and sobering fear that if we stepped out in faithful acts of service, we would likely be inviting new questions, challenges, and even resistance into our lives.

I couldn't argue with that. In my own faith, I have

experienced a journey that is messy and unpredictable. But I also knew that isn't a bad thing. I have come to know God more through struggle and spiritual wrestling during the night than through the bright sunshine of success. I wasn't alone. For many of the men in our group, God is more a God of questions asked in the depths of pain and uncertainty than a God of simple answers offered in times when life is on cruise control.

Our group discussed the resistance that would likely push up against our bold intentions of faithful service, and then committed to spending the next two weeks in prayer, waiting on God to clarify His desire for our actions.

The very next Tuesday at work, Tom was summoned to his manager's office and informed that he was being fired at will (he was quickly and completely exonerated from any shred of causality). He was escorted to his office by HR, given five minutes to clear out all of his personal possessions, and then ushered quickly and permanently out of the building and the company. Tom called me in tears from his car on the way home—confused, disoriented, angry, humiliated, and afraid—but sensing intuitively a direct connection between the bold pursuit of our group and this devastating life event.

After relaying the dizzying events he had just experienced,

his simple question was, "Can we just go back to reading books?" Of course, at this point the genie was out of the bottle. It was too late to re-cork our God-inspired desire to serve. That brought us back to the discussion of what new challenges and what resistance we might face in light of this desire to serve. Tom's situation ended up not dampening his or the group's enthusiasm but serving as a divine confirmation that we were on to something big and that our course was no longer the shoreline but deep waters. I'm sure Tom would have preferred another object lesson to illustrate how Satan will oppose God's plans, but his unwavering faith was an inspiration to all of us.

As time would reveal, Tom's experience would draw him and our whole group into much deeper water than we ever anticipated or would have even desired. The result was a far richer relationship with God in all of our individual faith journeys.

It would be much easier and safer to remain lukewarm, uncommitted, and risk-averse in our faith so as to avoid the pain and danger of crossing over to the other side. But it is just this attitude for which God reserves some of His most stinging judgment:

I know you inside and out, and find little to my liking.
You're not cold, you're not hot—far better to be either

cold or hot! You're stable. You're stagnant. You make me want to vomit. You brag, "I'm rich, I've got it made, I need nothing from anyone," oblivious that in fact you're a pitiful, blind beggar, threadbare and homeless (Revelation 3:15-17).

God's harshest judgment is for the sins of *omission* (when we fail to act) than the sins of *commission* (when we act but screw it up).

Tom learned to face his fears from the experience of being fired. He told us:

God grabbed me by the throat of my passive belief, claimed me, and made me declare my life for Him. He revealed Himself to me in a personal way that pierced my self-reliance, my need for status and my need for others' approval as being the most important things to me. Beyond all of this, God reassured me with the most profound learning—to stop being afraid!

God had called Tom to name the Isaacs of his life and sacrifice them on the altar of his unemployment.

No risk, no reward. But in between risk and reward is fearfully strong resistance. You can count on it. Resistance is often the confirmation that we are in the sweet spot of

God's will. Our greatest fear should not be that we encounter resistance. Our greatest fear should be that we are successful at something that does not matter to God. Perhaps the amount of resistance encountered is the gauge that registers the degree to which God celebrates our success—and Satan fears it.

God's *With-ness*

The reward for faithful risk is God's *with-ness*, especially in times of overwhelming resistance. St. Bernard Parish was among the hardest hit communities ravaged by Hurricane Katrina. The storm killed 114 people in St. Bernard and flooded every one of its 24,000 homes. The storm surge hit at 10:00 a.m. on August 29, 2005, and took only fifteen minutes to cover the parish in over ten feet of water.

Dorothy Hingle lit a candle sometime after 9:00 a.m. in her small brick house on Rosetta Street and prayed. She always lit a candle when she prayed. Dorothy spent her entire life in St. Bernard. At age eighty-three she was the matriarch of her large family of five children, fifteen grandchildren, forty-one great-grandchildren, and ten great-great-grandchildren. Most of her time was devoted to caring for her fifty-four-year-old stepson, Russell Embry, who had been paralyzed and severely brain injured in a 1974 accident. For thirty-one years, Dorothy had served as Russell's primary caregiver, bathing, feeding, and cleaning up after him.

Widowed in 1992, Dorothy had begun to be slowed by arthritis. She gave up driving and enlisted the help of others in caring for Russell. So complete was her devotion, however, that she seldom left his side, even to go to the grocery store.

Russell was 6' 4" tall and weighed 250 pounds. The combination of his size and impairment meant he was on a special needs list for those who needed to be evacuated in the event of a hurricane. As Katrina approached, Dorothy made arrangements for the ambulance to pick up Russell and her just as she had done in past storms. As the rest of the family fled, Dorothy assured them, "The ambulance is coming to get us. They're coming now. Don't worry about us. God is *with* us."

After Katrina's waters inundated St. Bernard Parish, there was no word from Dorothy or Russell. For the next twenty-four days, the family frantically searched hospitals, nursing homes, and the Internet for them. They supplied DNA samples and posted descriptions on forty websites, praying all the while that the ambulance had arrived in time.

As the water receded, searchers found Dorothy and Russell in their small brick home on Rosetta Street. Her purse was by the door in anticipation of their escape. The small candle was next to her. The wax had flowed out in a puddle beside her when the floodwaters washed over it. Dorothy and Russell died just as they had lived for thirty-one years—together. They lay together in Russell's bed with Dorothy's arms wrapped tightly around him, refusing in the face of the rising floodwaters to let go. God's grip on Dorothy strengthened her grip on Russell. I think of her as a Hebrews 11 hero of the faith.

If anyone had occasion to flee in the face of the rising waters of resistance, it was the apostle Paul. Wrenched from a career of killing followers of Jesus into a calling to reach the least, the lost, and the forgotten—the spiritual "cave dwellers" of his day—he endured whippings, shipwrecks, betrayals, stoning, hunger, and the desertion of earthly brothers in the name of Jesus for his efforts. In spite (or perhaps because) of all this, Paul was so completely confident of God as the eternal reward for his risk that he states:

> *I'm absolutely convinced that nothing—nothing living or dead, angelic or demonic, today or tomorrow, high or low, thinkable or unthinkable—absolutely nothing can get between us and God's love because of the way that Jesus our Master has embraced us (Romans 8:39).*

The reward for risking is God's all-powerful grip on us. Nothing, nothing, nothing can cause Him to let go.

While God's grasp never weakens, we must let go of all our excuses and distractions in order to wholeheartedly live out our faith. This is why Jesus knew he had to ask us the next question to enlarge and deepen our faith, a question intended to diagnose our spiritual health: "Do you want to get well?"

REFLECT AND RESPOND

READ the following Scriptures:

- Hebrews 11
- Romans 8:28-39

REFLECT on the following questions:

1. What is the "other side" of the lake for you?
2. How have you encountered resistance as you attempt to practice a bolder faith?
3. When have you felt God's *with-ness* in your life?

RESPOND to the following challenge:

- Choose one of Jesus' revolutionary teachings listed in this chapter—or elsewhere in the Gospels—and practice it for thirty days.
- Share with one other person the impact this has on deepening your faith.

Some time later, Jesus went up to Jerusalem for a feast of the Jews. Now there is in Jerusalem near the Sheep Gate a pool, which in Aramaic is called Bethesda and which is surrounded by five covered colonnades. Here a great number of disabled people used to lie—the blind, the lame, the paralyzed—and they waited for the moving of the waters. From time to time an angel of the Lord would come down and stir up the waters. The first one into the pool after each such disturbance would be cured of whatever disease he had. One who was there had been an invalid for thirty-eight years. When Jesus saw him lying there and learned that he had been in this condition for a long time, he asked him, "Do you want to get well?"

—

John 5:1-6, NIV

Chapter Three

DO YOU WANT TO GET WELL?

A QUESTION ABOUT WHOLENESS

Will I Ever Feel Healthy Again?

My wife Carol had been ill for over three months. What had begun as a slight discomfort in her lower abdomen had progressed to constant pain, rendering her unable to go about the active and healthy life with which she had been blessed all of her life. Simple daily tasks required more energy than she could muster. Her ability to work as a nurse became day-to-day, dependent on her energy and degree of pain. Carol considered taking a leave of absence rather than put the clinic in uncertainty over her availability on an almost-daily basis.

With her background in medicine and nearly two decades, experience in nursing, Carol is as good an advocate for her personal health as anyone I know. She asks the tough questions and speaks the mysterious language of medicine. Carol doggedly pursues doctors, nurses, and appointment schedulers until she successfully gets answers. In her lowest and most vulnerable moments, however, Carol was beginning to doubt that she would ever resume a healthy, pain-free life. She was facing the real possibility that she had entered this diminished state of being for the long haul—perhaps for life. When the deep discouragement of unanswered prayer washed over her, she cried out, "Will I ever feel healthy again?"

At no time during her ordeal did any of the physicians, specialists, nurses, lab technicians, orderlies, residents, or helpers turn to Carol and ask, "Do you want to get well?" To ask such a question would be somewhere on a scale between astonishingly insensitive and deeply disrespectful. What person, when dealing with a chronic, debilitating condition would *not* want to be restored to full health? Carol's constant prayer was for an immediate and full recovery. She was joined in that prayer by countless friends and family. No one would ever conceive of questioning her desire to be healed, to be made whole again.

Jesus' Unthinkable Question

In His perfect grasp of every life story, however, Jesus asked just that question to a man who had suffered constantly for almost four decades. Audaciously He asked him, *"Do you want to get well?"*

Maybe there were a few snickers in the periphery. How silly is that question?

It was the height of one of the Pilgrimage Feasts requiring all Jewish males to journey to Jerusalem. Jesus steps into the center of a throng of beggars of Bethesda and confronts this long-suffering man with His unthinkable question. He had the . . . insensitivity? rudeness? lack of awareness or perspective? . . . to question the desire of a man who had been an invalid for thirty-eight years. Thirty-eight years! For almost four decades this man had been huddled with the hundreds of sick people—blind, crippled, paralyzed—in the alcoves of the Sheep Gate pool of Jerusalem.

The superstitious belief of those trapped in this pitiful tangle of humanity was that periodically an angel of the Lord would come down, ripple the water, watch the mad dash to see who got in the pool first, and then grant healing to the winner. The worse off you were, the more you needed an angel's touch, but the less likely you would be first in the water. Too bad. Only the first person into the pool after the holy ripple would be cured of whatever ailed him. In the interim, the hundreds of alcove-dwellers would beg their daily subsistence from the residents and pilgrims passing by.

But why would Jesus question the man's desire to be made whole?

Perhaps the invalid trusted the healing power of the rippling water more than the righteous power of an Almighty God. Maybe he would rather have remained a comfortable beggar than a courageous kingdom-maker.

But maybe it's as simple as Jesus knowing that, to be healed, the man had a part to play.

A careful reading of the passage reveals that rather than *reaching out*, the invalid had become accustomed to *pressing in* to the shadowy recesses of the alcoves. He remained huddled with the hundreds of other forgotten and ailing men and women who had given in to the despair of long-unanswered prayers or to the predictability of subsistence living supported by the charity of those passing by. Bottom line, he had given up.

Before we get too judgmental and roll our eyes and write off this quitter, there are probably some problem areas of life where we have given up on the possibility of change, too.

Jesus was poised to transform all pain, heartache, and disappointment this man had endured based on his response to one unthinkable question: "Do you want to get well?" Jesus was also willing to give the man the choice to remain impaired if he answered no. He had to answer Jesus' question for himself, as do we all. My friend that I mentioned in the last chapter, Tom, e-mailed me his profound insights on Jesus' question to the man at the pool of Bethesda.

He seemed to be asking, "Are you sure that you are ready to have a radical redirection in your life? All of your excuses will be gone. Your limitations henceforth will be self-inflicted. You will have a world of new opportunities, new challenges, new demands, and new joys. Are you sure you're ready to leave your familiar and move into a new state of being?"

What about you and me? Do I want to get well? Do you want to get well? Are we ready for a new state of being? Do we dare to answer such a question by experiencing wholeness?

Null and Void

Webster's New World Dictionary defines *invalid* in the following ways:

in´va lid:

1. Not well; weak; sickly; infirm; chronically ill or disabled

2. To remove from active duty or retire because of ill health

3. Not valid—having no face; null or void

Are you feeling weak in body or spirit? Have you removed yourself from "active duty," choosing to press into the shadows of seclusion and self-sufficiency rather than step out into the light of community and commitment? Are you feeling as if you have no influence, no voice, as if your life right now is somehow of little value or effect? Does your life feel null and void?

The word that appears directly after invalid in the dictionary is *invaluable*.

in val´ yoo wa b´l:

1. Having value too great to measure

2. Priceless

None of us are invalids in God's eyes. We are all invaluables. True, we may indeed be sick or weak in body, crippled by debilitating disease or even approaching death. We may be chronically ill in spirit with patterns of self-defeating behavior that we cannot shake on our own, but we are priceless to God—of a value too great to measure.

Do you believe that? Do I believe that about myself? If there's even a shadow of doubt in your mind, consider different ways God thinks of us.

- We are the one lost sheep He hunts down, willing to ignore the ninety-nine others who require no such rescue. (See Luke 15:1-7.)
- We are the lost coin that He searches frantically for, turning over the whole house, as if we are the only thing of value He possesses. (See Luke 15:8-10.)
- We are the lost sons and daughters that He stands in wait for, despite the way we squandered all He had given us. He rushes madly to hug us when we stumble home. He throws massive parties on our behalf, clothes us in royal finery, and kills the best in the herd for us—just for showing back up. (See Luke 15:11-32.)

These storylines all move us deeply because we hunger to be loved, to be valued in such a way. And we are! We are so priceless that God offers up His most valuable asset—His only Son, Jesus, on our behalf in order to restore us to a love relationship and demonstrate our measureless value to Him. Invalid? No way! Invaluable? Without question!

But I Don't Measure Up

You are loved. Easy to understand but often a challenging truth to actually embrace and live. We get sucked into believing the lies perpetrated by slick marketing—and people who have hurt us—that we just do not measure up. We slip back into timid, fear-filled behavior and wither inside from a disease of the heart. We limp along at half speed or curl up half-heartedly in the shadows of the alcove. We stay on the surface and refuse to go deep in life and faith. It is all so much easier to quit than to say "yes" to a radical redirection—an uncomfortable and possibly dangerous prospect.

So Jesus' asks us, "Do you want to get well?" Embedded in Jesus' question about our physical health, we discover that godly healing is not just of body, but also of mind, spirit, and soul. And Jesus brings the same rhythm and sequence of his interaction with the man by the Sheep Gate to all areas of our well-being.

- There is Jesus' initial command to "get up"—to take action, to stop lying in the shadows, but to stand up, leaning on His steadying hand.

- There is His encouragement to "pick up"—to pick up only what we can carry, leaving behind all the baggage of wasted years, futile efforts, and fruitless self-dependence. We are to pick up only our mat, perhaps as a reminder that we were once sick but were restored to wholeness by His healing touch.

- Finally, there is His expectation that we "speak up." We are always healed for a purpose—we are blessed to be a blessing to others. Our own healing requires that we become the arms and legs and voice of the Great Healer in our world.

Jesus Takes the Initiative

The restoration of Carol's health began with a caring Mayo Clinic physician's question, "What is your story? Start at the beginning." Jesus skips right by this pleasantry with the invalid and with us. He cuts to the chase with His penetrating question, "Do you want to get well?" Jesus asks this question to draw us closer to Him. He requires us to weigh in for ourselves. But don't miss the simple truth that Jesus reached out to a man who had given up. Jesus spoke first.

The miracle of healing in John 5 is one of only two healings recorded in Scripture *not* initiated by an audacious act of human supplication and faith. The healing at the Sheep Gate pool, along with the miracle at Nain in Luke 7, stand in sharp contrast to Jesus' other miraculous healings. Why did He make His dealings with this man an exception?

Perhaps Jesus wanted to demonstrate that a small faith places no limits on His large plans, that knowing Him intimately is not a prerequisite for being healed by Him deeply. After all, Jesus said to His disciples when their faith was wavering, "I tell you the truth, if you have faith as small as a mustard seed, you can say to this mountain, 'Move from here to there,' and it will move. Nothing will be impossible for you" (Matthew 17:20, NIV).

Undoubtedly Jesus was showing His compassion. He knew He was dealing with a man who had lost almost all hope. That didn't exclude the man from daring to answer the question in his own heart—and pick up his mat. But be assured, when we have tapped out our own initiative, exhausted our own reserves, and doctor after doctor has raised her eyebrows and shrugged his shoulders in perplexed confusion, God steps in with His perfect timing and touches us with His gentle hand of healing. He does for us what we can't do for ourselves. Sometimes our faith stumbles to catch up to our prayers.

When we feel that touch, we must still be willing to break through our own spiritual inertia to go deeper in our faith. We must say yes to healing. If we are content to stay where we are, no healing can take place because we have, in essence, said no to it. God does not violate our free will.

William Barclay said of this miracle:

The power of God never dispenses with human effort. Nothing is truer than that we must realize our own helplessness; but in a very real sense, it is true that miracles happen when our will and God's power co-operate to make them possible.

Playing Small

"Are you as big as you want to be?" This pointed question was asked in a chance conversation with Blair, the CEO of one of our firm's clients. Caught a bit off guard by his directness, I popped in the mental tape from which I often described our company's business design. I began giving him my well-rehearsed answers. This time, however, they just did not ring quite true. I sounded hollow to myself.

We had somehow become accustomed to accepting our smallness. We even regularly described our firm as "small by design," as if this were a key distinguishing characteristic. Truth be told, we all desired to play and work bigger but lacked the vision, resources, marketing wisdom, and maybe even courage to grow beyond our self-imposed boundaries. As a result, we were certainly small but by default, not design. We were doing great work with select clients but lacked the scale to truly transform large numbers of people or whole global organizations.

God does not want us small by default. And this is certainly not His design. Militant modesty is not a God thing! Paul's encouragement to Timothy is God's instruction to us as well: "For this reason I remind you to fan into flame the gift of God, which is in you through the laying on of my hands. For God did not give us a spirit of timidity, but a spirit of power, of love and of self-discipline" (2 Timothy 1:6-7, NIV).

Jesus contrasts the desire of the thief (Satan), "who comes only to steal and kill and destroy," with His own ministry purpose: "I have come that they may have life, and have it to the full" (John 10:10, NIV). The thief's principal trick is to have us waste time—God's and ours—by playing small. The abundant life promised by Jesus is not necessarily a wealth of possessions but an overflow of influence—for God's sake. Erwin McManus says, "Jesus understood His purpose was to save us not from pain and suffering but from meaninglessness." It is a big life and deep faith He has in mind for us.

All of this requires that we first get up, that we break free from our comfort with whatever is shackling our spirit. To get up is an act of faith and hope. We must have faith that God will steady our atrophied spirit, shriveled from disuse. And we must have hope that the life to which we are called is greater than the one we leave behind.

Pick Up Your Mat

God's command to get up is followed by His encouragement to pick up our mat and walk. Why? If we no longer need our mat because God mercifully heals us, why not leave it behind for the next poor beggar? Does He know in His wisdom that we will need a reminder of our sickness that was transformed to significance?

Many years ago, at the wise encouragement of another father, I began taking one-on-one adventures with both of our sons at least once each year. I give them the opportunity to help plan and even pay a little bit, and we go off for several days of face-to-face, heart-to-heart, father-son time. It has become a vital part of the story of our relationship and the source of many belly laughs over the years!

The first such adventure was a backpacking trip with Brett in the Holy Cross Wilderness of Colorado. Neither of us even knew how to read a compass. I will never forget the scene in our living room as we laid out all the things we thought we required for our inaugural four-day foray into the back country—food (lots of it), clothes, first-aid kit, tent, sleeping bags, stove, rope, bug spray, flashlights—you get the picture. When we divided the stash and stuffed it all into our packs, they each weighed about sixty pounds. As I struggled to hoist Brett's pack onto his back, he looked at me with pleading eyes, suggesting that a hotel adventure was the way to go! We clearly needed to skinny down what we intended to carry, or we would be crushed by the weight of our packs about thirty steps from the car.

If we are going to be able to answer God's command to get up, we need to check out what we are carrying. The excess baggage of wasted years, futile efforts at self-healing or fruitless self-dependence are not trip essential. It weighs us down, threatening to crush us as we venture out from the shadows of the alcove into the light of a divinely healed life.

The things taking up space in our backpacks and our hearts can come in many forms—money, relationships, work, busyness, the guilt of the past, worries of the present or fear of the future. Anything that steals our heart away from faith weighs us down in our venture for God. The writer to the Hebrews said we are to "throw off everything that hinders" (12:1, NIV).

Jesus began His ministry with an invitation to His disciples and to us: "Come, follow me" (Matthew 4:19, NIV), and ends it with the powerful command to "go and make disciples of all nations, baptizing them in the name of the Father and of the Son and of the Holy Spirit" (Matthew 28:19, NIV). We can neither answer His invitation nor obey His command if we are frozen in our tracks by the weight of self-imposed burdens. We must be willing and able to pick up our mat.

The word for mat in the story of the beggar is "Krabbates," which is translated to mean "pallet." A pallet can have two quite different definitions, both applicable in our healing by God.

pal´it:

1. A platform for storing or transporting materials
2. A wooden tool used by potters for smoothing or rounding

In the account of John 5, the first definition most clearly applies. Others brought the invalid on a pallet to and from the pool on a daily basis. It was his only mode of transportation until Jesus intervened. But now his transportation was to become a tool in the hands of the Master Potter. Jesus used the pallet to shape the faith of the beggar—from invalid to invaluable, rounding off the dings and scuffs of thirty-eight years to become holy art for others to witness and marvel at.

Ultimately, that last point is why I believe Jesus asked him to pick up and carry his mat. It was much more than a reminder to the man of where he came from as he entered a new life. It was a prop, an ice-breaker, a conversation-starter that opened eyes and ears when he told the story of his miraculous healing.

Wounded Healers

We are healed always for a purpose. We are always blessed to be a blessing. I was constantly reminded of this vital truth in our Friday small group Bible study and fellowship time. God brought together twelve men who had the perfect stories and life experiences to be able to minister to each other in moments of darkness and need. But it required that we speak up.

Several years ago, in a moment of parenting despair, I reluctantly and tearfully shared my feelings of fear, anger and confusion with the group. Roger responded that he had asked his eighteen-year-old son to leave their house just the evening before. His son was near the bottom of a many-year struggle with drugs that was killing him and destroying the rest of the family. Returning late from a West Coast business trip, Roger felt compelled to kick his son out onto the street rather than allow him to continue to poison the family with his drug-induced dangerous and erratic behavior. Roger shared his story, admitting that the group was the last place he wanted to be that particular Friday morning. But he felt called by some odd force to be there—compelled despite a fear-filled, sleepless night. When I began to share my story, the reason for Roger's attendance became evident. He was there to speak hope into my despair and solidarity into my feeling of being all alone. One by one, several other men shared stories of how they too had reached moments of pain, fear, anger, and confusion with their teenage sons or daughters. They also shared examples of how many of those defeats had become victories over time.

Henri J. M. Nouwen describes what was taking place in his classic little book, *The Wounded Healer*:

Who can listen to a story of loneliness and despair

without taking the risk of experiencing similar pains in his own heart and even losing his precious peace of mind? In short: "Who can take away suffering without entering it?"

As we were leaving that morning, wrung out by the gripping stories of difficult life experiences but bolstered by the prayers and love of each other, one of the men pulled me aside and softly said, "John, we just became a group today."

We had been meeting for years—reading, praying, telling stories, complaining about the local sports teams—but seldom speaking up with real courage or transparency about the highs and lows of our lives. Until that morning. Speaking up opened the floodgates of reality. When we set down the façade of lives lived in relative order and daily calm, and began to share the truth, we began to become the group that God intended for us to be all along. He knit us together for just that morning—and for many more to come. Over the next four years, jobs were lost, health wavered, and our faith was staggered. In other words, life happened! And in every circumstance, there was more than one man who had experienced, or was currently experiencing, exactly the same reality. God's expectation is that we dare to answer with words of hope and comfort in these exact moments.

"As iron sharpens iron, so one man sharpens another" (Proverbs 27:17, NIV).

Paul was specifically chosen by Jesus Himself to take the Gospel beyond the Jewish nation. His credentials were dubious at best—by his own admission he was once "a blasphemer and a persecutor and a violent man" (1 Timothy 1:13, NIV). He stood by and watched as men stoned the Jesus-follower Stephen to death, a vision that was likely replayed in Paul's mind for the rest of his life. (See Acts 7.) Because of Paul's flawed and damaged past, he had a depth of understanding and empathy that allowed him to speak words of hope with passion and truth. His willingness to open up his life—the good, the bad, and the ugly—could not be quenched or quelled.

He explains his passion:

Christ Jesus came into the world to save sinners— of whom I am the worst. But for that very reason I was shown mercy, so that in me, the worst of sinners, Christ Jesus might display his unlimited patience as an example for those who would believe on him and receive eternal life (1 Timothy 1:15-16, NIV).

Or as Eugene Peterson states in *The Message*: "now he shows me off—evidence of his endless patience—to those who are right on the edge of trusting him forever." Paul was blessed to be a blessing.

God commands us to get up. Finally, because of His healing of us, He expects us to speak up. Paul understood this truth and made it part of his teaching:

He comes alongside us when we go through hard times, and before you know it, he brings us alongside someone else who is going through hard times so that we can be there for that person just as God was there for us. (2 Corinthians 1:4).

It's amazing what God can do in and through us when we say "yes" in response to His question, "Do you want to get well?"

Given our own healing, why would we limp along, hiding behind the pseudonyms of a previous life rather than boldly proclaim our true identity as a follower of Jesus?

Our next question comes from a confrontation between Jesus and a demon-possessed man. He asks that troubled soul and each of us, *"What is your name?"* in order for us to call out and claim our true identity. When we know our name, who we are, we are able to become active, redemptive, life-changing, and world-changing members of God's family.

REFLECT AND RESPOND

READ the following Scripture:

- Luke 15
- 1 Timothy 1:12-17 (Preferably in *The Message*)

REFLECT on the following questions:

1. Where are you currently "playing small" in your life, work, and/or faith?
2. What is currently weighing you down in your life and faith journey?
3. To whom are you feeling called to minister?

RESPOND to the following challenge:

- Inventory what you are carrying in your "backpack" the next thirty days and determine what, if anything—money, relationships, work, busyness, the guilt of the past, worries about the present, or fear of the future—is weighing you down in your pursuit of God and of others.
- Commit to sharing this inventory with one other person in an effort to rebalance your load.

They sailed to the region of the Gerasenes, which is across the lake from Galilee. When Jesus stepped ashore, he was met by a demon-possessed man from the town. For a long time this man had not worn clothes or lived in a house, but had lived in the tombs. When he saw Jesus, he cried out and fell at his feet, shouting at the top of his voice, "What do you want with me, Jesus, Son of the Most High God? I beg you, don't torture me!" For Jesus had commanded the evil spirit to come out of the man. Many times it had seized him, and though he was chained hand and foot and kept under guard, he had broken his chains and had been driven by the demon into solitary places. Jesus asked him, "What is your name?"

—

Luke 8:26-30, NIV

Chapter Four

WHAT IS YOUR NAME?

THE QUESTION OF IDENTITY

Monty's Relational Tapestry

O n the first night of every new class he taught, Monty would require the completion of a biographical form, including contact information and a family photo. One entire wall in his cramped office was covered with photos of past and present students. They were beginning to spill over to the adjoining walls. Black, white, brown; young, old; female, male; singles, couples, families; healthy, frail—the photographs created a visual tapestry representing decades of Monty's deep investment in the lives of others.

I received a preview of the kind of relationship I was to enjoy with him when I turned in my form and family portrait. Our family picture had been taken on a breathtakingly beautiful day somewhere in the Cascade Mountains. Because of the glare off of the snow pack, we were all wearing sunglasses. Monty looked at the picture, then up at me, inquiring with a mischievous grin, "Are you all in the witness protection program?"

What began as a nine-month Bible survey class blossomed over thirteen years into a deep, cherished friendship with Monty and, consequently, a closer relationship with God. Every time I met with Monty, he would pepper me with questions about my life, work, family, and faith. Often, the questions would come rapid-fire, five at a time, without even the courtesy of a pause for answers. Invariably, however, within the first couple of questions, watching my response, he would put his finger directly on something buried within my soul. Whether a passion, hurt, desire, doubt, or regret, Monty had a uniquely divine gift of revealing what was hidden, ignored, or barely scabbed over in the soul. He knew how to go deep.

I asked him on one occasion how he knew to ask the specific question that had, on that day, uncovered a long-unspoken fear. He replied that he had been praying for hours before I showed up—praying for me, by name—while looking at my family photo. These relationship-guided, love-filled prayers had the power to turn darkness to light, to take what was shallow into the deep, and to grant to anonymity its true name.

There was no witness protection program or any other kind of protection program we might erect that would guard your heart when Monty was around. If you dared sit down with him, you had best be prepared to be opened up by spiritual exploratory surgery. God's Word was the scalpel, and penetrating questions were his technique. Monty's inquiries quickly revealed both the reality of my situation and my true identity. I always left our times together with newfound clarity.

A Graveyard at Night

After a long day of telling stories and teaching timeless truths to countless people, Jesus called on His closest followers to join Him on a journey to the other side of the lake. (See Mark 4:35.) While the crowd remained on the shore, the little group set out to cross the Sea of Galilee at night. Given that several of Jesus' followers were professional fishermen, the night crossing of a notoriously fickle body of water was not the boldest part of Jesus' invitation. They knew how to handle a boat. The risk was not so much what they were *doing;* it was where they were *going.* The little band was leaving the devoutly Jewish region that had produced four of the twelve disciples to cross over to one of the poorest of Gentile regions. Their destination was directly opposite Galilee. This could not have been truer, both geographically and spiritually.

If the storm that almost drowned them en route was not enough to set off a panic attack, the group arrived at night to a welcome reception committee that consisted of one naked man, screaming at the top of his voice, chains hanging from his arms and legs. It is a scene straight out of a Stephen King novel, designed to speak directly to the mistaken self-perception and others-perception woven into the disciples' legalistic and judgmental faith. What could be worse for a Jew than being in an unclean burial ground at night, confronted by a naked man, who dwelled with the dead, while surrounded by rooting pigs? *Pet Cemetery* has nothing on this setting. It was the weirdest reception ever. Ever.

The setting was horror-movie perfect, but the story does not follow the predictable script. Three phenomena distinguish this most unusual encounter, all of which reveal the focus of our own faith. First, despite the creepiest of settings, Jesus remains perfectly calm. Amazingly it is the demons who are terrified. As was the case in the fierce storm during the lake crossing, Jesus is bold and unruffled. Because He is so in step with His Father—"I and the Father are one heart and mind" (John 10:30)—Jesus is fully confident that when He confronts evil, the God of heaven has His back. Do we access the same power by seeking the same solidarity with our loving heavenly Father?

Second, and equally astonishing, is the fact that even during this initial encounter, the demons know Jesus by name (Luke 8:28). After years of intimate friendship and daily walks of faith, the closest followers of Jesus still had to be prompted with the question, "Who do *you* say I am?" (Luke 9:20, NIV). This was not the case with the shrieking, blaspheming, furious, brooding agents of hell living inside and controlling the naked grave dweller. Speaking with the man's voice the demons acknowledged Jesus by name and by the rightful place He occupies in the universe: "Son of the High God."

Jesus' enemies are on a first-name basis with Him. Am I? Are you?

Third, and perhaps the most disconcerting turn of events, was that Jesus' first attempt at driving out the demons seemed to fail. This must have pulled His followers up short. Didn't

Jesus just muzzle a storm with one word merely an hour earlier? The followers, already terrified and wrung out from the storm, perhaps feared Jesus had used up all His strength on the lake. They had seen Jesus issue strong orders and drive out demons on every prior occasion, but this time, His words did not appear to be working. How far does His authority go?

Are we fully confident in God's resolve to *always* triumph over evil?

What's in a Name?

Jesus never wavered. He didn't turn from the tortured man in front of Him. Calmly, confidently, patiently—almost gently—He asked the same simple but probing question He asked throughout His earthly ministry and still uses today to call out our true identity and refocus our faith. He simply asked, *"What is your name?"*

If you were staring into the face of evil in a dark graveyard at night, would you ask the name of the ghoul in front of you? Would you take the time to introduce yourself? Or like me, would you be sprinting the other direction?

What is your name? Is that really important in this situation? Someone dangerous enough to be chained up by the local townspeople is dangerous enough to do you harm. Is his name the most pressing issue?

Further, wouldn't you think that the Creator of the universe, the God who has our hairs numbered and knows the flight path of every sparrow, would already know the man's name? I confess. I am terrible at remembering names. But shouldn't God be better?

Jesus asks, "What is your name?" not as a means of prodding His faulty memory but to force the man to confront his own identity. Once again, the question is not for Jesus' benefit but for ours. The question of identity is Jesus' divine methodology to challenge the man's self-destructive embrace of so many false identities and perceptions of the world. In the same way, Jesus asks us the question and challenges our own self-destructive embrace of our false identities and perceptions.

One need not be demon possessed to have constructed a world of devilish perceptions that destroy everything valuable in life.

Jesus asks us our name even though He already knows who we are—better than we know ourselves. That's the point. He wants *us* to become acquainted with *our* true identity. The demon-racked man in the graveyard had a whole Roman legion—6,000 evil, maddened screamers in his head—of false identities holding him hostage.

Living with Aliases

The world's population is roughly seven billion people. You may have seen this breakdown of demographics assuming that the entire world was represented in a village of 100 people:

- Sixty-one villagers would be Asian (of that number, twenty would be Chinese and seventeen would be Indian), fourteen would be African, eleven would be European, nine would be Latin or South American, and five would be North American.

- Eighteen villagers would be unable to read or write, but thirty-three (and counting) would have cell phones, and sixteen would be connected to the Internet.

- Twenty-seven villagers would be under fifteen years of age, and seven would be over sixty-four years of age.

- There would be an equal number of males and females.

- There would be eighteen cars in the village.

- Sixty-three villagers would have inadequate sanitation.

- Thirty-three villagers would be Christian, twenty would be Muslim, thirteen would be Hindu, six would be Buddhist, twelve would be non-religious, two would be Atheists, and the remaining fourteen would be members of other religions.

- Thirty villagers would be unemployed or under employed, while of the seventy who do work, twenty-eight would work in agriculture, fourteen would work in industry, and the remaining twenty-eight would work in the service sector. Fifty-three villagers would live on less than two U.S. dollars a day.
- One villager would have AIDS, twenty-six villagers would smoke, and fourteen villagers would be obese.

What stunned me is that sixty-seven villagers would have *no identity*. Of the almost seven billion people in the world, 4.6 billion are unknown in the sense that they have no published name, social security number, street address, or bank account. About 13.1 million adults were victims of identity theft in 2013. The 4.6 billion unknowns were not among them because there is nothing to steal. From a legal standpoint, it is as if they do not exist.

Now I know I am looking at identity from a Western literate perspective. The 4.6 billion with no official papers may have more of a sense of identity than some of us with birth certificates, driver's licenses, and passports. But the exercise of looking at the world in a single village made me wonder how many of the 100 know their true self.

A Cloak of Invisibility

There are times when I choose to be unknown. If I have been out all day or all week with people, I treasure being able to merely participate in something while letting others take the lead. I enjoy running and biking alone. This allows me to recharge and refresh. This is both a natural and healthy means for me to recover my energy, particularly for the introvert that needs alone time to recharge his batteries.

But becoming and remaining anonymous as a way of life—perhaps a self-defense mechanism to make sure no one hurts us again—becomes unhealthy when we have distanced ourselves from significant relationships and are a member of no community.

Erwin McManus writes, "Many of us live our lives making sure we are not seen. We choose the cloak of invisibility. We choose to remain uninvolved, and our love for personal privacy disguises both our indifference and our isolation."

Have you ever found yourself hanging back, saying no to interaction, not out of a desire to refuel but out of apathy or laziness? I have.

The tortured man in Luke's account was neither choosing

healthy anonymity nor personal indifference. He "had been driven into solitary places" by his demons. This is one of the evil one's favorite and most prevalent schemes—to make us feel all-alone, lacking a name or voice. We come to feel as if we are unknown even to the Almighty God. Satan has been at this game a very long time. He has this scheme down to a science. Tragically, we continue to fall for the lie that we have no name and no voice and that not even God knows where we have slipped between the cracks.

I grieve when I see a friend who is desperate for authentic human interaction draw back and shut the world out.

Fire from Heaven

Consider the ancient story of Elijah. In one of the most stunning reversals in all of Scripture, the prophet goes from the pinnacle of public victory to the pit of private isolation in just one chapter. Perhaps you know the story. (See 1 Kings 18–19.) Elijah challenges the whole people of Israel along with 850 prophets to declare their allegiance to the god who is able to rain down fire on an altar of wood and a sacrificial bull.

The prophets pray all morning. No answer. Elijah engages in some godly trash-talking, "Call a little louder—he is god after all. Maybe he's off meditating somewhere or other, or maybe he's gotten involved in a project, or maybe he's on vacation. You don't suppose he's overslept do you, or needs to be waked up?" (1 Kings 18:27). Nothing happens. Not a spark tumbles from the sky.

Then Elijah steps up, repairs the altar with twelve stones representing all of the tribes of Israel, cuts his sacrificial bull into pieces, and soaks everything with water until it fills the surrounding trench. In a culminating act that would make even an infomercial huckster or outrageous televangelist blush, Elijah calls but once on God to make His name known. Immediately, God's fire consumes the offering, wood, stones, dirt, and all of the water in the moat.

The people repent. The false prophets are slaughtered. God wins. Evil loses. But when Queen Jezebel, a Baal worshiper, hears what happens, she vows to have Elijah's head. Now I can understand him being frightened. But what he does next is perplexing. The man who had just stood boldly in the face of a mob of bloodthirsty enemies and skeptics hightails it out of town. Elijah flees into the sunset, never stopping to stand up to the evil queen armed in the glory of the victory God performed on his behalf.

After leading a country to repentance, we next find Elijah sitting under a tree slipping into the deep slumber of depression, hitting a low point where he contemplates suicide. What happened to our victorious hero?

In the space of only one chapter, the evil one, seemingly defeated on the mountaintop in front of hundreds of thousands of witnesses, was making a remarkable comeback. He isolated Elijah and had him convinced that he was "the only one left" (1 Kings 19:10) among all of the followers of God.

Before I become too self-righteous in my attitude toward the followers of the false prophets or judgmental about the doubts of Elijah, I need to recall my own experiences. I have to admit that I have felt the despair of unanswered prayer, even when reaching out to the real God. It has seemed, as with Elijah's taunts, that God was busy with other projects or taking an extended time away from my life. I can recall times when I cried out to God for a divine solution or powerful act and it seemed that all I heard in response was . . . crickets. Satan had me all alone without even the lifeline of prayer, or so it seemed.

Have you ever been there? Have you ever sat under the tree with Elijah? Have you ever cried out to God and heard nothing in reply?

A Quiet Whisper

There was much media fanfare when the biography of Mother Teresa of Calcutta was published: *Mother Teresa: Come Be My*

Light. What shocked reviewers and readers was learning that Mother Teresa spent the last half-century of her life tormented by the sense that God had abandoned her. This paragon of compassion describes her spiritual health using words like "dryness" and "torture." She wrote of reaching for God but finding only "darkness and coldness and emptiness so great that nothing touches my soul."

Like Elijah, she descended from the pinnacle of making God's love tangible to the sick and dying of Calcutta into a spiritual abyss of emptiness and isolation. Mother Teresa felt alone even as the religious order she founded touched the world with a message of compassion and hope.

To be sure, there are times that God calls His most faithful followers into what St. John of the Cross vividly described as "the dark night of the soul." The purpose of such a period is not to shackle us with fear but rather to free us for service. John writes:

> *What does the dark night of the soul involve? We may have a sense of dryness, aloneness, even lostness. Any over dependence on the emotional life is stripped away. The dark night is one of the ways God brings us into a hush, a stillness so that He may work an inner transformation upon the soul.*

God sometimes draws us closer with quiet. It was during Elijah's isolation that God calls to him, speaking in "a gentle and quiet whisper" (1 Kings 19:12). God asks Elijah, "Can you hear Me now?" paraphrasing the once popular cell phone commercial. Whether we are isolated by Satan's scheming or by God's governance, we need to hear the gentle and quiet whisper of our name in order to escape our anonymity.

Have you heard God's whisper lately? Are you listening? Do you dare answer?

The Call to Mentorship

My friend Keith recently commented that I was truly blessed to have had Monty as a "spiritual soul mate" for thirteen years. I agreed and would have been satisfied had he left it at that. But that's not how God works, is it? Keith continued by challenging me to aspire to a similar role in the lives of others, taking on the mantle of mentorship.

God was whispering my name, my true identity, through Keith, inviting me to step out of anonymity into a new identity as a lover and soul-mate of others. But here is the rub. My life's business card is already crammed with the identities of husband, father, family member, friend, business-owner, church-goer, small group leader, and so on. I would rather hide behind all of these other worthy identities than assume another challenging role.

The 4.6 billion unknowns are all intimately known by God. Fortunately, with God we are never anonymous, never without character or lacking a name. We are never truly isolated. We may, however, have far too many aliases that interfere with the true identity to which we are called.

The Shadow Man

Tom is one of the most creative men I know, so it came as no surprise when I asked him for a business card at the end of a lunch meeting, and he asked, "Which one?" He then produced three. It was a little unexpected, however, that the third card had a completely different name and title!

Recalling Monty's question, I teasingly inquired, "Are you in the witness protection program?" "Oh, no," he replied, "that's just my train name."

I can honestly say I had never heard that reply before. I had to hear what a train name was and to hear the rest of the story, but our time was up. Tom was happy to schedule our next meeting at a coffee shop in order to share the meaning of his third card.

Tom decided when he was twenty-nine to jump a freight train to the West Coast with two friends. They began their journey on a full moon evening in July of 1986, and rode boxcars from Minnesota to North Dakota, then on through Montana to Washington, finally ending up three days later in Seattle.

Adding to their epic journey, the three buddies assumed train names and fictitious professions. John, a retail broker, assumed his childhood nickname Jocko, later shortened to Ock, and became an unemployed hockey coach. Brian, a lawyer, became Spike, the writer. My friend Tom, an accountant, became Dusty. He later added his mom's maiden name Herold. His assumed profession was a photographer.

Why would the train name assumed by a twenty-nine-year-old adventurer still occupy the business card of a now fifty-year-old-business owner? Tom has succeeded at virtually everything he has tried in his professional life. He became a CPA in a Big Four accounting firm and was an owner, manufacturer, distributor, and then president and CEO of salon businesses in Minneapolis, Denver, New York City, and Italy. He currently owns a consulting practice.

Along the road of his life journey, Tom began to actively pursue his fictitious train profession of photographer. Using his pseudonym of Dusty Herold, he submitted pictures to the newsletter of his own salon company and began to exhibit an original collection of photos called the "Shadow Man."

When I inquired why he chose to disguise his true identity, Tom's answer was direct, "No one would have taken me seriously. To them, I was 'Tom the accountant.'" His fear was that the amazing photographic narrative, "Shadow Man," would somehow be diminished by his everyday identity of accountant, consultant, or CEO.

Am I the only one who finds the intersection of a fictitious name with an exhibit called "Shadow Man" to have a message of its own?

Wrestling with God

How many identities do you carry around? I go by many, depending on the situation. I am the husband of Carol and the father of two adult sons, Brett and Joshua. Add on business-owner, brother, family member, son, churchgoer, community member, and friend. But it does not end there. I am also backpacker, runner, cyclist, reader, writer, and more. Oh, I now have a newer identity I really like: grandpa! There is no font size small enough to fit all of these identities on one business card—at least not so anyone could read them with the naked eye. I am tugged daily in many different directions by each of these identities. Having this many roles inherently creates conflict among them as they vie for where I will invest my time, energy, focus, and money.

Don't get me wrong. These are wonderful identities. I am truly blessed to carry all of them. But in a sense they are all "train names," not the most important identity to which I am called.

When I have to fill out the immigration form while traveling outside the U.S., the form has a blank for my surname—my family name—and then for all of the given names on my passport. Given names represent a voluntary selection and often capture the hopes, dreams, and even history of a family. Maybe one of your given names comes from a special grandma or grandpa. We can have numerous given names, and sometimes even our family name changes with the addition of a hyphenation. If you have ever worked on your family tree, you might have come to a branch where the spelling of that name changed.

Then there are nicknames, which can be as simple as a shortening of the given name or a way to differentiate between a senior and junior. Sometimes a nickname tells more about a person than a given name. I knew a person who got the name "Sunshine," later shortened to "Sunny," in high school and that's who she's been known as for more than thirty years.

No matter what our family name or given name or nickname is . . . no matter how many names we have on our life business card . . . God has His own name for us. Our real name. The name that tells us who we really are.

When Isaiah attempts to comfort the nation of Israel in the face of the impending doom he has been prophesying of, he reminds the people that God knows their real name:

> *"Don't be afraid, I've redeemed you. I've called your name. You're mine. When you're in over your head, I'll be there with you. When you're in rough waters, you will not go down. When you're between a rock and a hard place, it won't be a dead end—Because I am GOD, your personal God, The Holy of Israel, your Savior"* (Isaiah 43:1-4).

I've called your name. By what name does God call you? Your first name? Your surname? Your nickname? Consider that it may not even be a name you currently recognize or use at all. To tell us who we really are, to announce a bold new undertaking, to reorient the direction of our life, God just might assign a new name to you. It would not be the first time He has changed the name of someone whom He is preparing to accomplish great things in His kingdom. Throughout biblical history there have been momentous and radical business card changes.

Abram, who already had an impressive name that

indicated he was a wealthy business-person, was renamed Abraham, which had an even greater meaning:

> *Then God said to him, "This is my covenant with you: You'll be the father of many nations. Your name will no longer be Abram, but Abraham, meaning that 'I'm making you the father of many nations. I'll make you a father of fathers—I'll make nations from you, kings will issue from you" (Genesis 17:3-6).*

Simon, a common fisherman, was renamed Peter, the rock, and became a catcher of men for God and a pillar of strength for the Early Church.

> *Jesus took one look up and said, "You're John's son, Simon? From now on your name is Cephas" (or Peter, which means "Rock") (John 1:42).*

Saul, the murderer of Christians, was renamed Paul and became God's greatest evangelist. (See Acts 13 for this subtle but profound name change.)

My favorite name change in the Bible? Jacob, a fraud and deceiver, became Israel, a man so desperate for change that he wrestled with God and would not let go. What a story!

> *The man said, "Let me go; it's daybreak." Jacob said, "I'm not letting you go 'til you bless me." The man said,*

"What's your name?" He answered, "Jacob." The man said, "But no longer. Your name is no longer Jacob. From now on it's Israel (God-Wrestler); you've wrestled with God and you've come through." Jacob asked, "And what's your name?" The man said, "Why do you want to know my name?" And then, right then and there, he blessed him. Jacob named the place Peniel (God's Face) because, he said, "I saw God face-to-face and lived to tell the story!" (Genesis 32:26-30).

All too often I identify with Jacob's first name. But I aspire to his second name, the name given to him by God. The Amplified Bible adds a powerful nuance to the story above. When asked his name by God, Jacob in the shock of realization of who he was whispers his ashamed reply, "I'm a fraud." God's loving reply was, "Not anymore."

God's desire is that we stop scheming and posing behind all of our given names. He blesses us when we wrestle with Him all night, refusing to let Him go.

What Is Your Real Name?

What is your real name? What if I told you that you and I have the same surname, a name that will shape our lives and provide us with the sense of purpose we have longed for?

I believe that it is only when we embrace our common surname of Jesus follower that we are prepared to fully become a member of God's family. If we accept the name that God has offered to us, we are blessed to inherit the family name of Jesus follower because of His great sacrifice for us. The beautiful passage from Isaiah 43 quoted earlier beautifully describes this glorious act of redemption:

I paid a huge price for you: all of Egypt, with rich Cush and Seba thrown in! That's how much you mean to me! That's how much I love you! I'd sell off the whole world to get you back, trade the creation just for you (Isaiah 43:3-4).

What an amazing thought. God would cash it all in—and, in fact He already has—just to allow you and me to draw closer and inherit the Family name and all that goes with it.

Abram got a new name, and it changed the course of his life. So did Jacob and Saul and Simon. How about you? How would your life change? Your words? Your purpose and goals? Your relationships? Your legacy? Your sense of identity? Would petty grievances bother you as much? Would you give up on a task you are called to because the going got tough? Would you relegate time with God to one day a week or a couple of minutes a day?

One unmistakable area of conviction for me is the realization that if God chases so relentlessly after me and gives everything—even His beloved Son—for my rescue, shouldn't I pursue others, those who are without spiritual hope and salvation, with the same passion and commitment?

Who do we know who needs to hear how much God loves them? Who do we know who needs to become a member of God's incredible family? Who will chase them if not us? Who else other than us, those who have become God's children and bear His name, will understand that their spiritual destiny is the most important matter in life?

Given our own God-gifted ancestry, whom are we being called to cozy up to next?

I need to hear God call me by my true name, Jesus-follower. Knowing who I am in Christ is my only hope of escaping the spiritual myopia where I am only able to see myself and my own life while missing completely the spiritual, emotional, and physical needs of the people who God places directly in my path on a daily basis.

Maybe you find yourself with the same near-sightedness. This is why Jesus asks us the next question in an attempt to restore us to the 20:20 spiritual eyesight He intends us to have: *"Do you see this woman?"*

REFLECT AND RESPOND

READ the following Scripture:

- 1 Kings 18:20–19:18
- Isaiah 43:1-4 (Preferably in *The Message*)

REFLECT on the following questions:

1. Do you ever choose to remain unknown? Invisible? Is this in an effort to refresh yourself or to allow you to remain uncommitted and uninvolved?

2. When have you felt isolated like Elijah? What did you do to break out of the darkness? How did God speak to you?

3. What are all of the identities that you carry around? Do any of them prevent you from drawing closer to God?

RESPOND to the following challenge:

- Take the next thirty days to assess which, if any, of your given names obscure the Royal Identity to which you are called.

- Commit to praying for how you can fully claim your family name—Jesus-follower—while living out the various roles in your life and work.

Now one of the Pharisees invited Jesus to have dinner with him, so he went to the Pharisee's house and reclined at the table. When a woman who had lived a sinful life in that town learned that Jesus was eating at the Pharisee's house, she brought an alabaster jar of perfume, and as she stood behind him at his feet weeping, she began to wet his feet with her tears. Then she wiped them with her hair, kissed them and poured perfume on them. When the Pharisee who had invited him saw this, he said to himself, "If this man were a prophet, he would know who is touching him and what kind of woman she is—that she is a sinner."

Jesus answered him, "Simon, I have something to tell you." "Tell me teacher," he said. "Two men owed money to a certain moneylender. One owed him five hundred denarii, and the other fifty. Neither of them had the money to pay him back, so he canceled the debts of both. Now which of them will love him more?"

Simon replied, "I suppose the one who had the bigger debt cancelled."

"You have judged correctly," Jesus said. Then he turned toward the woman and said to Simon, "Do you see this woman?"

—Luke 7:36-44, NIV

Chapter Five

DO YOU SEE THIS WOMAN?

THE QUESTION OF FORGIVENESS

Elvis's Call to Worship

It was over the top, off the map. It crossed . . . no, it obliter-
ated the line. A dancing Elvis in full regalia was gyrating to
Las Vegas show tunes to begin church this particular Sunday
night. We were not in Kansas anymore, nor in the Lutheran
Church of my childhood. I didn't even have to ponder for a
second to know I had never witnessed a call to worship quite
like this.

You could hear nervous snickering. Tense glances were

exchanged with each other. Is this okay? At church? Will he—or we—go to hell for this experience, in a church no less?

This was the fourth and final Sunday in a provocative series titled "God On Location," probing Jesus' teachings on the emotionally-charged topics of loss, power, and money set against the backdrops of New Orleans, Washington D.C., and New York. For this evening's teaching, Kurt, the director of the Upper Room Community, had flown with John, an intrepid cameraman, to Las Vegas to record people's perspectives on love—at 4:00 a.m. One after another willing participant brazenly voiced their version of the Las Vegas mantra, "What's done in Vegas, stays in Vegas," as an excuse for all sorts of immoral, foolish, and reckless behavior. It was actually quite fascinating, though I still couldn't wrap my head around the fact that I was viewing this saddest of reality shows in the sacred confines of our church.

This day, however, it was neither the dancing Elvis nor the sad social commentary captured on video that disturbed and still disturbs my soul. It was Kurt's show-stopping question that summed up Jesus' teaching. It's a question that still continues to haunt me.

There was a prostitute who observed them conducting all the interviews from a safe distance across the street. As Kurt and John were packing up in the wee hours of the morning, they decided to cross over to the other side of the street to gain one more perspective on love—that of a prostitute. As they cut across the intersection, she abruptly turned on her stilettos and ran away—in fear, shame, despair, not wanting to be revealed on camera, who knows what?

This epiphany moment caused Kurt to ask, first of himself and then of the assembled Sunday community, "What was it about Jesus that caused prostitutes *not* to run away?"

What indeed? Kurt was seeking to understand and then communicate the perspective of a God who draws in rather than drives away the marginalized.

"Do you see this woman?" In a blinding, dizzying instant, I clearly saw the prostitute across the street and was abhorred by my corrected vision—not of her but of myself. I am Simon in the story, questioning Jesus' judgment for interacting with an immoral person, all the while maintaining the front of being devoutly religious. In truth, until that moment I never really noticed that woman—nor countless other men and women like her. I still miss many of them today. My vision is often clouded by the cataracts of contempt and conceit— judgmental lenses on life that have been hardened by years of use. I am forgetful of the forgiveness granted to me for sins neither less nor greater than hers.

Jesus speaks directly and harshly on our judgment of others in His teachings from the hillside in Matthew:

"Do not judge, or you too will be judged. For in the same way you judge others, you will be judged, and with the measure you use, it will be measured to you. Why do you look at the speck of sawdust in your brother's eye and pay no attention to the plank in your own eye? How can you say to your brother, 'Let me take the speck out of your eye,' when all the time there is a plank in your own eye? You hypocrite, first take the plank out of your own eye, and then you will see clearly to remove the speck from your brother's eye" (Matthew 7:1-5, NIV).

Such a radical correction of vision requires more than mere contact lenses—it requires a spiritual corneal transplant.

What Do You See?

Jesus slices through layers of pride, contempt, and even embarrassment with His penetrating question of vision: "Do you see this woman?"

I read the words of this passage. I answer the question, "Of course I see her." But Jesus' question does not allow me to stay on the surface. He is not asking His disciples or us if we experience an appropriate biological response to the visual stimulus of a woman in the center of the drama. He is asking if we see this woman in the same way He sees her.

As with the other questions posed by Jesus, I discover that when my heart is open, it is not me who is reading the Bible—it is the Bible reading me.

Until the instant of that question, Simon, the wealthy and generous host, a man interested in this Galilean teacher, apparently doubted the prophetic power of Jesus—"If this man was the prophet I thought he was . . . "—and Simon was surely defensive at having the town whore cause a scene at his house party—"he would have known what kind of woman this is who is falling all over Him" (Luke 7:39). Had he known this was going to happen, Simon might not have invited this unpredictable and controversial rabbi. He was undoubtedly wishing the woman would vaporize so he could get on with impressing his neighbors. This was . . . awkward.

An intimate encounter with Jesus is not something we get to manage. He takes the lead. The experience is always deeper, richer, fuller, more unsettling, and unpredictible than we could ever anticipate. It makes no difference why we seek Him out or why we invited Him over to our house for dinner. If invited, Jesus accepts. And it is always an eye-opening experience. He uses the occasion to invert our intentions and radically redirect our life. With Simon, it was the perfect opportunity to teach him (and us) about forgiveness, a lesson he . . . we . . . I . . . so desperately need to learn over and over and over again.

Seeing the Invisible

As part of an annual leadership series I facilitate for county employees, we always tour the facility in which the class is being held. Last year, it was the new city jail. On that particular day, the jail housed 845 people—from men and women just passing through for twenty-four hours or less to people who would remain there or a similar facility for years.

Our guide simulated the sequence of events prisoners experience upon arrival at the jail. We began in the bowels of the building, where prisoners entered the facility and proceeded through intake and pat down, clothing issue, finger printing, booking, the "one phone call" booths, mug shot stations, and finally to processing. We observed exercise facilities with a basketball hoop and small roof windows to allow tiny shafts of natural light to penetrate the surreal surroundings. There were small concrete cells for prisoners who could not co-exist with others and cavernous rooms filled with prisoners watching TV, playing cards, or reading.

Throughout the tour, I had a growing sense of heaviness in my soul. These men and women were, in many cases, the least, the lost, and the left out, products of generations of poverty, abuse, neglect, and abandonment. It is a vicious cycle of petty crimes to felonious behavior passed on from one generation to the next. The guards knew many of the inmates by both name and pattern of behavior because they had been in this prison dozens of times before.

I felt compassion, but, honestly, I was more relieved that the doors separating us from the prisoners were all locked and that I was visiting for a mere hour. The windows had thick shatterproof glass so I could not hear the thoughts of my imprisoned brothers and sisters. It made it somehow easier to file silently past the cells and avert my gaze from the inmates' looks of anger, curiosity, hatred, longing, surprise—to not see them as men and women just like me. And yet I felt an overwhelming sense that the line separating them from me was razor-thin. A different circumstance, choice, upbringing, mentor, spouse, or day—and I could easily have been one of them. There, but by the grace of God, go I.

When we returned to the classroom, I looked quietly at the twenty-five somber students and finally asked, "How do you feel?" One woman's answer reflected my own emotion: "I feel disoriented."

I had not only lost my physical sense of direction while walking for an hour through the maze of an eight-story windowless prison; I had also become aware of my own spiritual blindness through seeing these imprisoned people.

It would be easy to slide past prisoners in jail, never having found ourselves behind bars; to glide past prostitutes on street corners, never having sold our bodies for cash; to ignore immigrants because we grew up here; or to disassociate with the elderly because we still feel young. But then we encounter Jesus.

Jesus always acknowledged the overlooked, loved the unloved, and clearly spied the invisible:

- He saw the two sets of brothers, Simon and Andrew and James and John, who were bored with their job but hungered for a calling.
- He saw Matthew the tax collector in his booth and Zacchaeus the chief tax collector in his tree.
- He saw the woman who had been bleeding for twelve years and the woman who had been crippled by a spirit for eighteen years.
- He saw the faith of the men who dropped their friend through the roof and the faith of the widow who dropped two coins in the temple basket.
- He saw his disciples straining at the oars because of the wind and the rich young man straining at life because of his wealth.

A Divine Field of Vision

Luke's account of this dinner, featuring the town whore, is a perfect setting for Jesus to display His divine field of vision. A memorable cast of characters was all present. First, we have a snobby, self-righteous host. If we turn this into a movie, we might want to play him with an upper crust British accent. Then, there is a room full of spectators, thinking they could see what was going on but actually blind to what was right in front of them. Since they aren't the stars, we'll just cast them from a pool of extras. But then there is the woman. The femme fatale. She is "a woman who had lived a sinful life in that town." She is trouble from the start. She is a notorious character, an outcast, and a sinner right from their midst.

Who are you in the drama? The snob? The crowd? The sinner? What is disturbing to me is that I can see myself in every cast member. Maybe you have the same feeling.

The prostitute's lifestyle had escaped no one, certainly not Simon, whose revulsion of her was expressed in the judgment of his thoughts: "If this man [Jesus] was the prophet I thought he was, he would have known what kind of woman this is who is falling all over him." I can imagine his thought process. A good man wouldn't let this kind of woman touch him. I think Jesus is probably a pretty good man, so that means He can't be a prophet or He would know what was happening. He's actually a little naïve. We'll joke about this later—after He leaves. This gullible rabbi from the boondocks is getting hoodwinked by a promiscuous woman of the night. If He only knew, I'll bet He would jump right out of His skin.

Simon may have been urbane and savvy, but he certainly didn't have the 20:20 vision the prostitute was graced with. She timidly approached Jesus, staying behind Him and then kneeling at His feet. Why behind Him? Was it just the logistics of the table? I suspect it was because she was too humiliated and fearful to look Him in the eye. Kneeling at his feet she showed the extent of her humility. This isn't quite the bold, flirtatious character we were expecting from this kind of a woman.

She knew He knew who she was, what she had become. It wasn't the life she expected as a bright-eyed little girl. It wasn't the life she wanted. She didn't sniffle a little as she began to anoint Jesus with perfume. The baggage of her brokenness caused her to sob profusely, "raining tears on [Jesus'] feet" (Luke 7:38).

What she did next probably caused an audible gasp in the room filled with men. She let down her hair. William Barclay, in his book *The Gospel of John*, explains that it was "an act of the gravest immodesty. On her wedding day, a

Jewish woman bound up her hair and never would she appear with it unbound again. The fact that this woman loosened her long hair in public showed how she had forgotten everyone—except Jesus."

She could not even utter a confession. All she had were tears over a life of poor choices and bad living. Aren't you thankful that when we have been in the same place as the woman, when we didn't have the words to say, God heard us anyway because "the Spirit himself intercedes for us with groans that words cannot express" (Romans 8:26, NIV).

Only when we are brutally honest and own up to our own pathetic condition—when we bend broken at Jesus' feet, rain tears of remorse, and let down our hair—will we understand fully our own desperate need for forgiveness. And only then will we have eyes that are open spiritually. Now we are finally prepared to answer Jesus' question. Now we are ready to go deeper with God.

Penniless and Without a Plan

There were more than seven million personal bankruptcies filed in 2005—and about another million are filed each year since then. The average age of the applicant was thirty-eight. Forty-four percent of filers were couples, thirty percent were women filing individually, and twenty-six percent were individual men. Two out of three filers had lost a job. Half had experienced a serious health problem. This number increased daily in the recession of 2008.

The spiritual reality is that 100 percent of us have to file for personal bankruptcy with God. Whether married, single, or divorced; young, middle-aged, or old; healthy or ailing; employed or not. Regardless of our economic worth, we do not have the personal worth to buy our way out of this brokenness. We are penniless and without a plan.

Jesus awakens Simon to this truth in His teaching on forgiveness: "Two men were in debt to a banker. One owed five hundred silver pieces, the other fifty. Neither of them could pay up, and so the banker canceled both debts. Which of the two would be more grateful?" (Luke 7:41-42).

Neither man had the money to buy his way out of debt. That is our reality, too, isn't it? We really don't have the cash either. We are bankrupt—borrowing, as the saying goes, "against money we do not have, to buy things we do not need, to impress people we do not even like!"

William Cope Moyers, vice-president of Public Affairs and Community Relations for Hazelden, recalls the moment life recovery began for him:

I folded my arms over my chest, longing for comfort, for peace. I was so sick—so sick and tired of it all. In that moment I realized the hopelessness of my situation, and in a sudden, brief flash of clarity, I asked myself, "Now what?" I stared at the filthy wood floor littered with half-empty beer cans, cigarette butts and used syringes. The answer wasn't here in this room any more. It was all over. I was done."

Like William, we deceive ourselves with excuses, religion, friendships, family, health, and good intentions. In the end, though, all of these things we try to bring to the table are worthless, insufficient collateral to purchase freedom from our addiction to sin. We are broke.

God's great missionary, Paul, had to admit to the same bankruptcy:

I've spent a long time in sin's prison. What I don't understand about myself is that I decide one way, but then I act another, doing things I absolutely despise. . . . I decide not to do bad, but then I do it anyway. My decisions, such as they are, don't result in actions. Something has gone wrong deep within me and gets the better of me every time. It happens so regularly that it's predictable. . . . I've tried everything and nothing helps. I'm at the end of my rope. Is there no one who can do anything for me? Isn't that the real question? (Romans 7:14-15, 19-21, 24).

Paul reaches the only conclusion possible: he is wretched, miserable, despicable, contemptible—he is bankrupt.

One of Satan's favorite schemes to damage our spiritual journey is to overwhelm us with the crushing weight of our debt—even after God has forgiven and forgotten it. John warns us that Satan is a liar: "When he lies, he speaks his native language, for he is a liar and the father of lies" (8:44, NIV). He loves to tell the lie that we are hopeless, that we can never get out of hock.

Looking back at his lowest moment in that filthy room, William Cope Moyers learned and teaches that "any hope worth experiencing is the hope that follows the loss of hope." It is vital to note that William is not referring to *all* hope but the *false* hope placed in drugs, alcohol, money, looks, business, fame, friendship, and even family or religion. All of these are hopeless at the end of the day to buy us out of the spiritual debt we have piled up through sin.

The Language of Hope

God's native tongue is different than Satan's. It could not be more different. It is a deep heart language whose dialect is *hope*:

- "No one whose *hope* is in you will ever be put to shame" (Psalm 25:3, NIV).

- "He will not grow tired or weary, and his understanding no one can fathom. He gives strength to the weary and increases the power of the weak. Even youths grow tired and weary and young men stumble and fall, but those who *hope* in the Lord will renew their strength. They will soar on wings like eagles; they will run and not grow weary, they will walk and not be faint" (Isaiah 40:28-31, NIV).

- "Now faith is being sure of what we *hope* for and certain of what we do not see" (Hebrews 11:1, NIV).

What are we hoping for? There is no future in "Buy now—pay later. No money down and zero interest until eternity." The bill will come due sooner or later. And, we will not have more collateral than we do now. We will still be bankrupt.

Thank God the story does not end here. Jesus finished His story with the words of hope we desperately need to hear: "So the banker canceled the debts of both."

Amazing Grace

Mark Early graduated with a law degree from William and Mary and was in private practice for fifteen years. For the next ten years, he was a Virginia state senator and then served one term as attorney general of the Commonwealth of Virginia. Mark described his role as "spending a lot of time figuring out how to put more people in prison and then keep them there longer."

After running unsuccessfully for governor in 2001, he was approached by Chuck Colson to be his successor as CEO of Prison Fellowship Ministries. Mark's initial response was brutally honest: "Why would I invest in prisoners at the midpoint of my life? If I invest in anyone, they would be people with resources, with reputations, with a standing in the community. Prisoners have no hope and no future."

But as he read his Bible, Mark began to discover God's upside-down economics. He encountered Moses, a fugitive from justice after killing an Egyptian and then burying his crime in the sand. This was the same Moses that led his people from captivity.

He met Paul, the man specifically called by Jesus to carry His story beyond the Jewish world but also a man who today would be tried, convicted, and sentenced to prison as a co-conspirator in the murder of Stephen.

Mark began to understand that God takes the very people we would throw away—the ones who seemingly have no value—and raises them to be great leaders in His community and kingdom. The worthless become priceless. Sometimes they are the ones who make the most powerful difference in the lives of others. It is precisely because of what characterizes their past that their present and future become such powerful testimonies of amazing grace.

In February of 2002, Mark Early was appointed president and CEO of Prison Fellowship, a ministry that has been running for four decades, communicating the message of God's hope and forgiveness to inmates in all fifty states and more than 115 countries.

Jesus' first miracle was one of compassion for a wine-broke groom who was about to suffer the humiliation of his social miscalculation. Jesus' greatest miracle is one of love for all of us who are life-broke, having insufficient collateral to buy our way out of spiritual bankruptcy. Jesus offers up His own life as a full payment for our debt. In one amazing act, He picks up our tab and offers us new life and new hope.

Jeremiah saw this day coming when he spoke in God's voice to the people: "I know what I'm doing. I have it all planned out—plans to take care of you, not abandon you, plans to give you the future you hope for" (Jeremiah 29:11).

So what do we do with all of this? When we are awakened to our blindness and convicted of our bankruptcy, when we catch a hint of the vast sum paid to bust us out of our sin's prison, how do we respond? How do we answer Jesus' question?

The point of Jesus' penetrating question in Luke 7 is giving and receiving forgiveness. He wants to soften our lens on life so that we see our brothers and sisters—*all* of our brothers and sisters—with eyes refocused by forgiveness.

Simon thought he was the one who saw life clearly and that Jesus was missing the drama unfolding before Him. Nothing could have been further than the truth. It was Simon who needed his vision corrected. Jesus doesn't mince words or hold rebuke from Simon, but isn't it good to know Jesus cared about him in his lostness, too?

Simon, I care about you so much I don't want to see you lost. Let me explain . . .

"Do you see this woman? I came to your home; you provided no water for my feet, but she rained tears on my feet and dried them with her hair. You gave me no greeting, but from the time I arrived she hasn't quit kissing my feet. You provided nothing for freshening up, but she has soothed my feet with perfume. Impressive, isn't it? She was forgiven many, many sins, and so she is very, very grateful" (Luke 7:44-47).

We, too, have been forgiven many, many sins. Our only response is to be very, very grateful, expressed in loving God and forgiving others.

And how do we love each other? It begins by being Jesus for people. When we are cut off on the freeway, we forgive. When we are victims of gossip, we forgive. The anecdote for angry words is forgiveness. The response to devious business dealings is to forgive again. This is not the economic formula of the world that seeks to repay bad deeds with retribution and retaliation. This is not a tough-guy slogan like: "I don't get mad, I get even!" This is God's economy, which requires that we *be* Jesus because we *see* Jesus in all of our brothers and sisters. We forgive because we were forgiven.

John Newton's beloved hymn celebrates our new eyesight: "Amazing grace! How sweet the sound that saved a wretch like me. I once was lost, but now am found, was blind, but now I see.

The dictionary defines "blind" as

blīnd

1. Sightless
2. Unable or unwilling to perceive or understand
3. *Botany.* Failing to produce fruit

When we choke the flow of forgiveness in our lives, the first two definitions are obvious: we don't see and are unable to perceive or understand. But the third definition, from the science of botany, also applies spiritually. If we are blind to our own brokenness, unwilling to perceive the needs of others, we will be unable to produce the fruits of the Spirit in our own lives.

Forgiveness is something we do for others, but ultimately it boomerangs and showers blessings on us as well.

As we are lavished with the gifts that accompany forgiveness, do we seek to unload some of our undeserved gain on others, or do we hoard the benefits for ourselves? Jesus continues to deepen our faith journey with His next question, which is intended to unleash godly generosity, *"How many loaves do you have?"*

REFLECT AND RESPOND

READ the following Scriptures:

- Matthew 7:1-5
- Romans 7:15-24 (Preferably in *The Message*)
- Isaiah 40:28-31

REFLECT on the following questions:

1. When have you had an eye-opening glimpse of God's forgiveness like Kurt?
2. When have you intentionally averted your eyes from seeing someone else?
3. How have you personally experienced God's native language of *hope*?

RESPOND to the following challenge:

- Focus the next thirty days on *forgiving*—when cut off on the freeway, when the victim of gossip, when underappreciated, when on the receiving end of a tongue-lashing or the silent treatment—forgive! Every time.
- Make notes throughout the next thirty days on ways God brings forth new fruit in your relationships and in your soul.

By this time it was late in the day, so his disciples came to him. "This is a remote place," they said, "and it's already very late. Send the people away so they can go to the surrounding countryside and villages and buy themselves something to eat." But he answered, "You give them something to eat." They said to him, "That would take eight months of a man's wages! Are we to go and spend that much on bread and give it to them to eat?" "How many loaves do you have?" he asked.

—

Mark 6:35-38, NIV

Chapter Six

HOW MANY LOAVES DO YOU HAVE?

A QUESTION ABOUT WEALTH

The Third Offering

Nathan was our guide, driver, and interpreter. He and his wife Sarah, along with their children, served as missionaries translating the Bible into the Likoni dialect with the Konkomba people of Ghana, West Africa. On this particular morning, he was giving us a crash course on the Ghanaian church while swerving his Toyota Land Cruiser through the chaotic streets of Accra, choked with potholes, people, and vehicles of every kind. One of the things he told us was that, unlike a typical church service back home, there would be two offerings instead of one. Knowing that we had exchanged minimal U.S. dollars into Cedis, the local currency, he suggested we consider holding a little back from the first offering in order to be able to contribute to the second. He didn't want us to be embarrassed.

The service began like services I've attended in the United States. There was a familiar liturgy, hymns that I grew up with, and an order of service that reminded me of countless other Sundays. The choir, resplendent in crimson robes adorned with gold stoles, sang a beautiful anthem following the pastor's message. The first offering was like any other collection I had experienced—the wooden plate was passed down the rows of people, into which the bills and coins representing some percentage of a weekly wage were deposited. I felt confident contributing a few Cedis, knowing that I had several left in anticipation of the second offering.

Shortly after the plates had been brought to the front of the open-air sanctuary, the choir began singing what I can best describe as a spiritual mambo. The singers began to slowly weave their way from the back of the church to the front, gathering people from the pews along the route, to become part of a beautiful community ribbon of worshipers celebrating God's goodness. While the first offering was a restrained, five-minute affair, the second was a forty-minute wild celebration of God's blessing with singing, dancing, clapping, and rhythmic movement that swept the whole church up into the presence of the Spirit. People came forward with coins and bills. Those with neither offered open hands as a testimony of their willingness to give fully of themselves. I snaked my way forward with the throng, thankful for a few Cedis in my pocket to drop in the plate but also feeling the stirrings of conviction. The Holy Spirit was nudging me gently and then more firmly, beginning a personal transformation that would upend me from a lifetime of stinginess into a deeper understanding of true wealth and generosity.

Eventually, the service returned to a flow that I was more accustomed to—hymns, prayers, and the approaching benediction. Whew! That had been uncomfortable. Time to get back to normal.

Before I could settle back into the safe zone of familiarity, however, there was a rustling in the back of the church as a news crew arrived, equipped with cameras and microphones. My colleagues and I were summoned to the front. With cameras rolling and microphones extended, we were presented with a $2,000 check and a humble apology. I'll never forget the words:

We're so sorry. This is all we can give. We know it's not much. But when we saw the suffering our brothers and sisters in New Orleans endured following Hurricane Katrina, we suffered too. We entrust you with all we could gather up in these past two weeks to help them out.

This third offering was from a 200-member congregation in the heart of a city with 70 percent unemployment and manual laborers earning an average of one dollar per day in wages.

Goodbye comfortable and normal. I was wrecked! As the presentation unfolded, all I could do was weep. This third offering cut to the very core of my selfishness. While I held back a few Cedis in order to smugly contribute to the second offering, my brothers and sisters in Accra gave—not generously or even sacrificially—but foolishly by the world's standards, from wells that held no water and wallets that contained no money. They were boldly living out God's audacious dare, the only dare contained in scripture: "Test me in this and see if I don't open up heaven itself to you and pour out blessings beyond your wildest dreams" (Malachi 3:10).

Is it any wonder why the Christian Church in this African country is experiencing explosive growth and blessing? Is it any wonder the Christian Church in America is in decline and continues to slip into the margins of popular culture?

Jesus' Testing Question

Our two sons were both home from college several summers ago. Their presence had a huge impact on our grocery bill. At 6' 5," our younger son Joshua is like a park bear, scavenging the refrigerator and cupboards for food 24/7. When Carol and I were on our way out to do the weekly grocery shopping—now a daily task—we would do a verbal inventory with the boys: "Do we still have milk? Lunchmeat? Yogurt? Cookies? Bread? Cereal?"

When Jesus asked the disciples, "How many loaves do you have?" He was not putting together a shopping list to keep the refrigerator stocked with both necessities and comfort foods. And even if the question seems preposterous with 5,000 hungry mouths to feed, He wasn't being sarcastic or making a joke. Jesus was testing His followers—including us—to force us to identify the level of our trust in the power of His provision.

Be aware that God is doing just fine without us. Speaking through a song of David, God declares:

I have no need of a bull from your stall or of goats from

your pens, for every animal of the forest is mine, and the cattle on a thousand hills. I know every bird in the mountains, and the creatures of the fields are mine (Psalm 50:9-11, NIV).

John's account of the same event we read in the Gospel of Mark tells us that Jesus "already had in mind what he was going to do" (John 6:6, NIV). Everything was under control. His question was not based on finding out if He what He needed to perform a miracle. It was a probing, challenging question to help us understand and measure our own faith through the lens of Godly stewardship.

Stewardship Is Not a Bad Word

Whoa! Let me stop right there for a moment. "Stewardship?" It's not a particularly appealing word today. It doesn't stir hearts or inspire us to go deeper in our walk. In fact, sometimes stewardship is a downright repellent word. It evokes negative images. The word and the concept have a bad reputation—perhaps well-earned and deserved. But the word stewardship is not loved, in large part, because of the human condition—our inclination is toward selfishness.

No wonder stewardship—a concept that is essential to God—doesn't come up in church much anymore. When stewardship is preached and taught on an annual Stewardship Sunday—a cue for some churchgoers to schedule a trip to the lake—it is often dumbed down to mean mere financial management, ignoring the most important dynamic: radical trust in God's goodness.

Stewardship committees conduct annual stewardship campaigns to drum up support for church budgets and programs. Just the word *campaign* should be our first hint that we are way off track. Following Jesus is never a singular campaign but always a way of life, a daily walk. But perhaps the biggest clue that we've missed the boat on stewardship is the first and possibly only word that popped into our minds when we read the word on the page. Money. We are to be wise stewards of everything, not just money.

Wesley Killmer offers a wonderful corrective and enriching definition of the stewardship:

> *Stewardship is God's way of raising people, not man's way of raising money. God's ways are often about challenging and reshaping our values, our worldview. Fundamentally in life, we don't do what we believe. We do what we value.*

By asking His testing question, Jesus was zeroing in directly on what His disciples valued, on what we value. He was making us declare in public what most of us prefer to leave private: the state of our finances in relation to our faith. But then He is the God of incisive inquiry. He is drawing us closer, inviting us to go deeper, by asking a penetrating question about what occupies the throne of our heart. Do we dare answer Him?

Jesus did not shy away from the topics of money, possessions, wealth, or stewardship. In fact, He taught more on this subject than any other, except the kingdom of God.

Why? Was it because He was addressing wealthy suburbanites who had a lot to manage? Hardly! With a few notable exceptions, the followers most drawn to Jesus were among the poorest people in the peasant class. They were unemployed and many were unemployable. They were common laborers, at best, but were just as often the beggars and outcasts.

Does Jesus ask what we have because He needs to raise funds to support a staff and building campaign? Surely not. The disciples were unpaid volunteers and Jesus was nomadic, journeying from town to town to live out His calling. He described his living arrangements by saying, "Foxes have holes and birds of the air have nests, but the Son of Man has no place to lay his head" (Luke 9:58, NIV). Jesus spoke openly and often about wealth because He knew that possessions pose a huge spiritual problem for us. Is it any wonder Satan loves to use finances to tempt us away from our heart's desire to live for God? Satan would love to keep us from going deeper in our spiritual walk by exploiting the prevailing views of wealth. Satan is so confident that money is the road to spiritual shipwreck that he even used the glory of wealth to tempt Jesus:

> *For the third test, the Devil took him to the peak of a huge mountain. He gestured expansively, pointing out all the earth's kingdoms, how glorious they all were. Then he said, "They're yours—lock, stock, and barrel. Just go down on your knees and worship me, and they're yours" (Matthew 4:8-9).*

How we deal with what we have tells a deep and consequential story about us. It reveals the condition of our heart and the depth of our trust.

True Wealth

Jesus knew that when He asked, "How many loaves do you have?" the disciples' response would disclose their lack of faith in His unlimited capacity to accomplish His work—and care for their needs. It created for them (and for us) a teachable moment, revealing that our hidden desire to withhold—even if we are only holding back a few crumbs and sardines—is our biggest deterrent to realizing true wealth. Money can either be a significant impediment or powerful accelerant to our intimacy with God.

It is crucial to note that the miracle of the feeding of the 5,000 is the only miracle, other than Jesus' resurrection, to appear in all four Gospels. That fact alone should indicate to us that stewardship is not a mere annual campaign but an essential truth of what it means to follow Jesus. If we get the answer to Jesus' testing question right in our heart—not just our head but in our heart—the tumblers of many other life questions will begin to click into place.

What about you? Are you, like the disciples, feeling the pinch of self-imposed scarcity? Not the true poverty of not having enough to eat but the gnawing neediness of always wanting a little more. Are you incredulous that Jesus would request a pattern of giving that goes well beyond generous or even sacrificial to outright foolishness? Do you often feel yourself holding back—giving in to the worldly guidance to "pay yourself first"?

I'm not just posing those questions to you. I am with you in feeling the tug to want more for myself. I cannot tell you how many times I sang the old hymn, "Take My Life and Let It Be," growing up. The fourth verse reads, "Take my silver and my gold, not a mite would I withhold." What I can tell you is how many times I have actually *lived* this verse. It would not take both hands to add it up!

So let us journey together—this is a tough climb, and we will need each other to make the ascent—as Jesus reverses our feeble interpretation of stewardship and our fearful attitudes toward money. He alone is able to flip our scarcity-minded withholding to a richer, deeper experience of true wealth. The result will be a new abundance within our spirit that gives not from what is left but to Whom is first. Stewardship. This is the crucial next step on the path to a deeper faith.

Start with Honesty

From the first day we were married, Carol and I co-mingled our funds. We have joint checking and savings accounts. Our only individual savings are for retirement and a checking account I use to pay business expenses.

Carol is our money manager out of necessity—we learned early it is just not my sweet spot. This became abundantly clear when the initial statement from our joint checking account arrived in the first month of our marriage. I gave it a cursory glance and quickly tossed it into the garbage. Carol, with a look of stunned horror, dove head first into the can after it.

"What are you doing?" was her incredulous question. I

knew I was in trouble but tried to stay cool. My off-hand response was, "The same thing I've done with my own individual statements for years. If we're out of money, the bank will let us know."

My days of managing our family finances were finished almost as soon as they started.

I do not share this with great pride. Having one person in charge has worked for us but is not a textbook best practice for managing financial tension in a relationship. There are plenty of good reasons why you might choose a different strategy. What I can tell you is that openness and honesty about our finances—from the spending to the making to the giving and the belief system—is imperative in our marriage, and I can't recommend the same approach to you strongly enough. If money is the biggest cause of conflict in marriage, then better to get everything out on the table rather than let problems, conflict, and misunderstanding fester.

Carol and I can still experience a great deal of emotional tension fueled by money matters, even after thirty-five years of marriage, but thankfully that is the exception and not the rule. We stumbled into the truth that transparency and honesty, particularly in money matters, helps dissipate a lot of stress in a relationship. Withholding information, obfuscating, and keeping secrets is always destructive, not just in a marriage relationship, but in our spiritual relationship with God.

As we dig deeper into stewardship, can we start there? Can we commit to being open and transparent? Can we admit if we're stingy, selfish, and miserable and not try to sweep the truth of where we are under the rug? This isn't doing God a favor. He already knows our heart. This is for our benefit.

One of the most unique and compelling stories of the early church was tied to transparency and money.

> But a man named Ananias—his wife, Sapphira, conniving in this with him—sold a piece of land, secretly kept part of the price for himself, and then brought the rest to the apostles and made an offering of it. Peter said, "Ananias, how did Satan get you to lie to the Holy Spirit and secretly keep back part of the price of the field? Before you sold it, it was all yours, and after you sold it, the money was yours to do with as you wished. So what got into you to pull a trick like this? You didn't lie to men but to God" (Acts 5:1-4).

The sin of Ananias and Sapphira was not how much or how little they gave to the church—but lying to their brothers and sisters in Christ, lying to themselves, and most of all trying to lie to God.

Selfish Withholding

Jesus set up His miraculous meal by asking a question that required honesty and revealed the condition of the heart. But let's move into the miracle itself. Why is it so important that it appears in all four Gospel accounts? And for inquiring minds, how in the world did five loaves and two fish satisfy such a large gathering?

One of the things that makes the story so important is that it is a precursor to the Last Supper of Jesus and His followers, where He tells them His body will be broken and His blood will be spilled as a sacrifice for the sins of the world. The feeding of the 5,000 powerfully foreshadows the Last Supper with a prayer of thanksgiving followed by the breaking of bread that nourishes both physically and spiritually. I believe that is one of the reasons it is united with the Resurrection as the miracle that appears in all four Gospels.

That's why it's so important. But how did it happen? The simplest explanation is that the event was a miraculous multiplication of matter. Jesus exercised His power to exponentially grow five loaves into a bread factory and two fish into a hatchery, generating enough food that thousands were fed in one sitting—with leftovers to take home.

I believe in miracles. I believe God has the power to intervene supernaturally into what we call the natural world. With God, every option is on the table. But there is one more way to look at this miracle that I find both fascinating and personally convicting. We are told that when Jesus told His followers it was time to get away from the crowd so they could rest and grab a bite to eat, word got out as to where they were going, and thousands of people streamed ahead to meet them. While Jesus was sailing across four miles of becalmed water, the crowd was running ten miles around the top of the lake. William Barclay describes an intriguing way that the miracle might have unfolded:

> *There is the crowd; it is late and they are hungry. But was it really likely that the vast majority of that crowd would set out around the lake without any food at all? Would they not take something with them, however little? Now it was evening and they were hungry. But they were also selfish.*

The disciples, when encouraged by Jesus to feed the hungry crowd, responded with scoffing, "Are you serious? You want us to go spend a fortune on food for *their* supper?"

(Mark 6:37, italics added). Their cynical solution was to "pronounce a benediction and send these folks off so they can get some supper" (Mark 6:36).

The disciples weren't alone in looking out exclusively for themselves. Is it possible that most of the entire 5,000 were true to the human condition of withholding from others to protect themselves and hid their food from everybody else to make sure they had enough? It is in the Gospel of John that we discover the source of the five loaves and two fish:

> One of the disciples—it was Andrew, brother to Simon Peter—said, "There's a little boy here who has five barley loaves and two fish. But that's a drop in the bucket for a crowd like this" (John 6:8-9).

Again, is it possible that the courageous act of one little boy who refused to horde the meal his mother had packed for him sparked an outpouring of sharing and generosity in the crowd? Could that be the miracle? Could it be that when we finally realize God's resources are unlimited and we have everything we need and begin to give, we experience the miraculous power of God in our lives and the world around us?

The world's wisdom is that what we have is ours. We have earned it. We own it. Our time is ours to spend; our money is ours to invest. We have the right to keep it and control it. Save, don't give—especially not to strangers. There's no Return On Investment in that!

This is exactly the conventional wisdom that Jesus seeks to radically reverse with His penetrating question on what we have. He uses the most available props and the least willing participants to showcase His path to true wealth.

Wealthy in What Matters

God wastes nothing. He wants us to internalize every nuance of this miracle because every detail informs how we are to steward wealth as a follower of Jesus. Let us look together and learn from the specifics of the story:

The Resourcefulness of God

"Here is a boy with five small barley loaves and two small fish, but how far will they go among so many?"
John 6:9, NIV

Barley was the bread of the poor and was further held in contempt because it was often the food offering of a woman caught in adultery. The fish were pickled sardines, likely carried by the boy to help choke down the dry barley bread.

Jesus begins His teaching with a graphic picture of how

He can and does work with anything. Anything. He is reminding His followers and us that an impoverished adulterer's gift, when put to Royal use in the service of others, is immeasurably more valuable than anything we might squirrel away, no matter how fast, shiny, sexy, expensive, or large. Five puny rolls and two pickled fish are the core of an upside-down understanding of stewardship as a Jesus-follower.

The Abundance of Community

*Jesus got them all to sit down in groups of fifty or a hundred—
they looked like a patchwork quilt of wildflowers
spread out on the green grass!*
Mark 6:39

Church is always community. I love how the Lord's Supper is celebrated at Park Avenue Church in South Minneapolis. The people of that community gather on both sides of the rail in front of the church, shoulder to shoulder, facing each other as they receive the bread and wine. You cannot help but *see* each other, *smell* each other, *feel* each other. It is an intimate meal shared by members of the same family.

Big screen Power Points, choreographed one-hour worship, massive weekend conferences, celebrity pastors and mega-church madness, individualistic worship that is a spectator sport—all can lead us from the power of community. The body Jesus was awakening was a rag-tag collection of selfish losers whom He grouped shoulder to shoulder in fifties and hundreds. They ate together, completely satisfied, as they began to break the bread that was multiplied, including that which they themselves had been withholding from their neighbor. The miracle happened in community because the Bread of Life inspired them with barley loaves and fish from a small boy.

Eugene Peterson's vivid description of the 5,000 as a patchwork quilt of wildflowers is wonderfully reminiscent of Jesus' teaching on worry and generosity from His Sermon on the Mount:

> *Instead of looking at the fashions, walk out into the fields and look at the wildflowers. They never primp or shop, but have you ever seen color and design quite like it? The ten best-dressed men and women in the country look shabby alongside them (Matthew 6:28-29).*

The largest, most well-orchestrated mega-church service looks pretty shabby next to a community of fifty fully committed to sharing barley loaves with each other, too!

The Power of Gratitude

Taking the five loaves and the two fish
and looking up to heaven,
he gave thanks and broke the loaves.
Mark 6:41, NIV

Jesus, who was present when everything was created—*Everything was created through him; nothing—not one thing!—came into being without him* (John 1:3)—still has a deep personal appreciation that everything is God's and therefore gave thanks for the gifts of mere barley loaves and sardines. To forget the Creator, the Owner, the Giver of all things is ungrateful arrogance.

In *Blue Like Jazz*, Donald Miller tells the story of a friend who rakes him over the coals for complaining he did not have enough money—while at the same time admitting to giving very little away:

That is not your money. That is God's money. You ought to be ashamed of yourself stealing from God and all. You write Christian books and everything, and you're not even giving God's money back to Him.

Jesus was modeling the consistent and persistent Old Testament call to acknowledge God as provider and not fall into the sinful arrogance of believing the good life is due to our own efforts and abilities:

Make sure that when you eat and are satisfied, build pleasant homes and settle in, see your herds and flocks flourish and more and more money come in, watch your standard of living going up and up—make sure you don't become so full of yourself and your things that you forget God, your God (Deuteronomy 8:12-14).

Moving toward a radical understanding of stewardship begins with the realization that God desires to use everything and everybody, working together in selfless community, fueled by thanksgiving.

The Influence of a Few Common Men and Women

Then he gave them to his disciples
to set before the people.
Mark 6:41, NIV

Participants at the National Prayer Breakfast are greeted each year with a little pamphlet titled *The Strategy of Jesus*, which contains these words from Elton Trueblood's 1947 lecture, "A Radical Experiment":

Jesus was deeply concerned for the continuation of His redemptive, reconciling work after the close of His earthly existence, and His chosen method was the formation of a small band of committed friends. He did not form an army, establish a headquarters, or even write a book. What He did was to collect a very few common men and women, inspire them with the sense of His spirit and vision, and build their lives into an intensive fellowship of affection, worship and work. One of the truly shocking passages of the Gospel is that in which Jesus indicates that there is absolutely no substitute for the tiny, loving, caring, reconciling society. If this fails, He suggests, all is failure; there is no other way. He told the little bedraggled fellowship that they were actually the salt of the earth, and that if this salt should fail there would be no adequate preservative at all. He was staking it all on one throw.

With the crushing volume of need in the world today, we are God's plan. He always works through people. He must. God has no Plan B. He gives us the bread and fish and then waits to see whether we distribute it or tuck it deep into our own pockets. We must answer His question of wealth and provision with our actions.

The Secret of Contentment

They all ate and were satisfied, and the disciples
picked up twelve basketfuls of
broken pieces of bread and fish.
Mark 6:42-43, NIV

The result of true wealth is contentment. Now there is a word seldom spoken. When was the last time you uttered the words "I'm so satisfied" or "I'm absolutely content" in conversation? The very concept of being content has taken on the negative connotation that you are a slacker.

There were twelve basketfuls of fish and chips, one for each of the reluctant disciples, after the feast was over. No one was questioning whether there was enough for everybody anymore. What a testimony of God's power to fully satisfy. Paul writes of this supernatural satisfaction in his letter to the Philippian believers:

Actually, I don't have a sense of needing anything personally. I've learned by now to be quite content whatever my circumstances. I'm just as happy with little as with much, with much as with little. I've found the recipe for being happy whether full or hungry, hands full or hands empty. Whatever I have, wherever I am,

I can make it through anything in the One who makes me who I am (Philippians 4:11-13).

Do you want "the secret"? The real secret? The ultimate secret of contentment? I do! Let's forget the best-selling book by the same title. Paul poignantly and personally revealed the secret centuries ago: "I can do anything through him who gives me strength" (Philippians 4:13).

The miracle of feeding 5,000 people is not one of mere multiplication—though five loaves and two fishes were transformed into a feast. The miracle is also the softening of selfish hearts, where people stop clutching what they have and share with those around them. True wealth, in God's upside-down world, is only accomplished and experienced in and through His body of followers who give sacrificially—and sometimes foolishly—of their wealth and most of all themselves to others. Only God can take us deeper and create the miracle of changing our withholding into wealth; our temptation to conceal into contentment.

So what do we do with the twelve baskets of leftovers? It is just this concern that Jesus seeks to address with His next penetrating question, *"Will you give me a drink?"*

REFLECT AND RESPOND

READ the following Scripture:

- Mark 6:35-44
- Deuteronomy 8:2-5, 10-20

REFLECT on the following questions:

1. Where are you currently withholding your money, time, or giftedness?

2. If "God's ways are fundamentally about reshaping our values, our worldview," how does He need to reshape yours? How is He currently doing just that?

3. Why do you believe Jesus spoke so often and so openly about money?

RESPOND to the following challenges:

- Endeavor the next thirty days to be deeply thankful. Start and end each day with an extended time of thanksgiving, for gifts large and small. See how this practice impacts your faith journey and your sense of true wealth.

- What is something special to you that you have held onto so tightly it is a burden rather than a blessing? Would you be willing to give it away? Make that a matter of prayer and thought the next thirty days.

The Pharisees heard that Jesus was gaining and baptizing more disciples than John, although in fact it was not Jesus who baptized, but his disciples. When the Lord learned of this, he left Judea and went back once more to Galilee.

Now he had to go through Samaria. So he came to a town in Samaria called Sychar, near the plot of ground Jacob had given to his son Joseph. Jacob's well was there, and Jesus, tired as he was from the journey, sat down by the well. It was about the sixth hour. When a Samaritan woman came to draw water, Jesus said to her, "Will you give me a drink?"

—

John 4:1-7, NIV

Chapter Seven

WILL YOU GIVE ME A DRINK?

THE QUESTION OF GENEROSITY

Shopping for Curtains

Every July our church sponsors a series called Summer Voices. This is an opportunity for people from outside our community to share how God is challenging them as activists and leaders in this season of their life. Sandra was the first to share her heart last summer. She is a part-time pastor at a North St. Paul church and director of The Lift, a non-profit that works with at-risk students. Several years ago,

Sandra and her husband felt called to move from the suburbs into the city to live out their faith in a visceral way.

I must admit that, for the first part of her talk, I was guilty of CPA—continuous partial attention—"uh-huhing" a lot of her experiences and intellectually agreeing with her assertions but not totally engaged. My head was in it, but my heart was miles away.

But then Sandra stopped and shared a series of questions that had caused her to do a 180 on faith and hunger.

"Suppose," she said, "that you were going to buy new curtains for your house and someone next door was starving. Is it okay to still buy the curtains?" No brainer, I thought. Of course not!

"But what if that person lives at the end of the block? Then what?" Well I suppose I'd pitch in, I thought.

"What about just in the neighborhood?" Now this was getting tougher. I don't know all the people in my neighborhood. How would I know? Would I care?

"How far away does the person have to live before it's okay to buy curtains and *let them starve to death*?" she asked. Now Sandra had my full attention. Her summer voice was rattling around my head and had spread throughout my being. Now it was reverberating in my heart.

What little we hear about the poor in the U.S. often

refers to them as a group, species, or statistic from some distant land. In truth, 24,000 people die each day from hunger or hunger-related diseases, one every 3.6 seconds. But they do not die as a class. They perish one at a time—as brothers, sisters, fathers, mothers, daughters, sons—leaving behind heart-broken families attempting to carry on in extreme poverty while coping with deep grief.

Alexandr Solzhenitsyn, in his brilliant Nobel Lecture in Literature from 1970, makes this pointed observation:

We confidently judge the whole world according to our own home values. Which is why we take for the greater, more painful and less bearable disaster, not that which is in fact greater, more painful and less bearable, but that which lies closest to us. Everything which is further away, which does not therefore threaten this very day to invade our threshold—with all it's groans, it's stifled cries, it's destroyed lives, even if it involves millions of victims—this we consider on the whole to be perfectly bearable and of tolerable proportions.

I have become quite accomplished at bearing groans and stifled cries as long as they aren't close to home. Perhaps it is a defense mechanism so as to not be overwhelmed by the news of typhoons ravaging, earthquakes burying, and hurricanes devastating, more often than not, the poor in places that seem distant and remote. I don't dare utter the prayer of Bob Pierce, founder of World Vision and Samaritan's Purse: "Let my heart be broken with the things that break the heart of God." Truthfully, I'm terrified of the consequences of such a request. I tend to cover my eyes and protect my heart from seeing or feeling the hungry, parched, or poor.

Is it any wonder I am suddenly moved to go shopping for curtains? Maybe I can pull them tight so I don't have to see the plight of a hurting world.

God Is in the Slums

Jesus never averted His eyes or heart from the poor or suffering—He never pulled the curtains tight and pretended that pain and suffering wasn't part of life. In fact, throughout Scripture and in the world today, the poor and suffering are God's primary focus.

Irish pop star and humanitarian Bono put it powerfully: *God is in the slums, in the cardboard boxes where the poor play house. God is in the silence of a mother who has afflicted her child with a virus that will end both of their lives. God is in the cries heard under the rubble of war. God is in the debris of wasted opportunity and lives and God is with us if we are with them.*

John's account states that God *had* to go through Samaria. Geographically, this made sense. But culturally there was no imperative to take the road through Samaria. To the contrary, there was an imperative to avoid it like the plague.

Palestine, where Jesus was working, was approximately 120 miles from north to south, and consisted of three distinct regions: Galilee in the north, Samaria in the middle, and Judea in the south. The quickest route from Judea back to Galilee was directly through Samaria—a trek of about three days. Because of a bitter racial feud dating back over seven centuries, Jews would take the bypass around Samaria and venture along the Jordan River—just outside of Samaria—to re-enter Palestine in Galilee. That meant they doubled their travel time, but their feelings of superiority were well protected. The extra travel day kept them insulated from contamination with the impure Samaritans.

As we discovered in the way Jesus treated the prostitute who anointed Him with perfume, Jesus saw the world much differently. The key understanding of national identity in the Old Testament was expressed by Moses: "Move back from the tents of these wicked men! Do not touch anything belonging to them, or you will be swept away because of all their sins" (Numbers 16:26, NIV). That theme was echoed throughout the first five books of the Bible. And truly, there are evil activities and people we must avoid. Paul counsels us to be cautious even when we minister to a brother or sister who has fallen away from the faith: "Brothers, if someone is caught in a sin, you who are spiritual should restore him gently. But watch yourself, or you also may be tempted" (Galatians 6:1, NIV).

But Jesus points to a new day of worldly interaction by His actions and when He commanded His followers to, "Go into all the world and preach the good news to all creation" (Mark 16:15, NIV). Jesus' imperative is our imperative: we must go to all the world with a message of hope and redemption.

Just a Little on the Trashy Side

When Jesus set out through Samaria with His disciples it would seem He was ducking out of trouble that the Pharisees were stirring up in His ministry. But Jesus was no coward who shied away from conflict. He stepped squarely, boldly, purposely into a far bigger controversy by leading His small band of followers directly through Samaria—the Badlands. To make the story more outrageous, Jesus posed the question of generosity—a question we must all dare to answer—to a *Samaritan woman* . . . who had been *married five times* . . . and who was now living with a *sixth man*.

There's an old Jerry Jeff Walker hit song where one of the bad boys of country music declared, "I like my women just a little on the trashy side." You might have heard it even if, like me, you don't listen to country music. It's got a great melody, and it is sung with a twinkle in his eye and big dose of humor, even if "trashy" isn't the way most women—or men— want to be thought as. In Jesus' day—and probably our day—the Samaritan woman at the well fit that description perfectly.

Let me break this journey and this encounter a little further. First, rather than choosing the respectable and religiously correct route, Jesus strides directly into the home territory of racially impure half-breeds, the Samaritans. Half-breeds. Ouch. There He speaks to a woman at a Jewish landmark, Jacob's well. To have a holy spot defiled by such a person would have infuriated the righteous of Jesus' day.

But don't skip over the fact she was a woman. Philip Yancy says:

In those days, at every synagogue service, Jewish men prayed, "Blessed art Thou, O Lord, who hast not made me a woman." Women sat in a separate section, were not counted in quorums and were rarely taught the Torah. In social life, few women would talk to men outside of their own families, and a woman was to touch no man but her spouse.

Jewish rabbis, in particular, were never to speak to a woman in public, not even their wife, daughter, or sister.

Segregated, not allowed to vote, no access to education, women truly were second-class citizens.

But not to Jesus. Not even if they were Samaritan. Not even if they were five-times divorced and living with a sixth guy.

As if to put an exclamation point on His scandalous behavior, Jesus speaks to a woman who is alone. How inappropriate. Particularly a woman with her reputation. It appears that she was shunned even by the women of her town. There was a well in the middle of Sychar, but she chose—or was forced—to walk the half-mile to draw water outside the city. She was alone rather than with other women of Sychar. She was there in the mid-day heat rather than at dawn or dusk, the normal times to fulfill this task. The whole setup points to a woman filled with shame, loneliness, and rejection. Interestingly, theologians and pastors over the centuries seem far more interested in her marital status than Jesus. He clearly saw someone through whom He could work, then and now.

The first person with which Jesus chooses to reveal the secret of His true identity and to ignite a revival in a long-scorned region was this five-times-married Samaritan woman.

Jesus starts a revolution by asking for *her* help and in so doing opens *our* eyes to the reality of true generosity.

Can You Spare a Drink?

Are you guarding your heart from the ravages of world disasters or from the poor—and maybe immoral—just down the street or a short drive across town? Have you become skilled at bearing the cries of distress that echo all around you? Are the cries of today's Samaritan women muffled by miles or diminished by distance? Jesus moves from our heads to our hearts with His question, "Will you give me a drink?" It jars us out of our spiritual lethargy and teaches us that any request for basic needs can be a divine call from God Himself to respond generously with mercy, justice, and humility. He seeks to turn upside down our narrow focus from getting to giving—even giving the smallest amounts of our most basic gifts. Will we give Him a drink? Our answer to this critical question deepens our faith.

Rolls Royce Religion

Running through the Minneapolis airport years ago, my attention was grabbed by the *Time* magazine on the newsstand display. "Does God Want You to be Rich?" asked the lead story. The provocative cover art featured the grill of a Rolls

Royce with a cross as the hood ornament. The article was a description of the new gospel of wealth—also dubbed the "prosperity gospel" or "name-it and claim-it theology." Of Christians surveyed, only 17 percent said they considered themselves part of this movement. But 61 percent believed that God wants people to be prosperous and 31 percent— almost a third of American Christians—concluded that if you give your money to God, He would bless you with more money in return.

I know that hard work coupled with opportunity will often lead to prosperity. I have also experienced firsthand that when we bless others we can't stop blessings from coming back to us—and sometimes those blessing are financial and material. God honors work. God blesses His people. I have no fight with that.

But to build a belief system based on a God who focuses on financial blessings—especially when the God of the Bible calls us to self-sacrifice and to lay down our lives for others— is problematic in its construction and expectation. What of the heroes of the faith we read about in Hebrews 11? Serving God was not a get-rich plan for their lives. Yet the Gospel of Prosperity is alive and well and is especially seductive as the world's economy heads south or lurches sideways. Lear-jetting telepreachers paint Jesus as a sort of blessed byway to the five Cs of the materialistic life: clothes, cars, cash, clubs, and credit. I know that some of these ministers are personally generous, but philosophically and theologically, their way of helping the poor is to "encourage people not to be one of them."

The lure of this message turns former NBA arenas into mega-churches and sells millions of books. This is all very interesting but directly opposed to Jesus' point of view and call to action.

When Jesus delivered His first temple talk back in His hometown of Nazareth, He announced the mission for His entire ministry. It was clearly not a message of today's "name-it and claim-it" theology. He names the focal point for His blessing—"God's Spirit is on me; he's chosen me to preach the Message of good news to *the poor*, sent me to announce pardon to *prisoners* and recovery of sight to the *blind*, to set the *burdened and battered* free" (Luke 4:18, italics added). And His claim is one of compassionate and sacrificial action, right here and right now—"*This* is God's year to act!" (Luke 4:19, italics added). Jesus' message was so well received that His own townspeople tried to throw Him off a cliff! A similar message today may net the same result. Maybe I need to rewrite this book and promise the reader health and wealth.

Our natural desire—not the same as the true desire of

our heart—is for a gospel message that is softer, easier, and more affirming of human selfishness. That allows us to close the curtains on the needs around us. We would rather shield our eyes from the poor, continue to forget about the imprisoned, and let the sinner die in is sins without a message of hope. We're fine with an occasional field trip to see how *those people* live and offer up a quick prayer for the burdened and battered. But really act? Not so much! The claims I stake are often for my own interests. My prayers, too often, are for more blessings to be heaped on my already abundantly blessed life. This is not the generosity of which Jesus speaks.

Bold Actions, Not Mere Words

Jesus was quoting from Isaiah 61 when He stated His ministry's purpose. This chapter in the Bible follows closely behind one of the clearest descriptions of godly generosity. Isaiah 58 is titled "True Fasting" in most translations, but it is also a perfect account of the unselfishness that only God can inspire.

This is the kind of fast day [generosity] I'm after: to break the chains of injustice, get rid of exploitation in the workplace, free the oppressed, cancel debts. What I'm interested in seeing you do is: sharing your food with the hungry, inviting the homeless poor into your homes,

*putting clothes on the shivering ill-clad, being available
to your own families (verses 6-7).*

This vivid portrait is easy to envision but very demanding to practice.

The best way to learn is to teach—and the most powerful way to teach is to embody the message in bold actions, not mere words. I would rather see a sermon than hear one any day.

Bob's Camp Out

Eighteen years ago, the owner of a small shoe repair shop named Bob Fisher began living out a sermon for the working poor and marginalized people in his community. In a moment of dubious sanity, he decided to take up winter camping in Minnesota, a state that frequents the Weather Channel. Bob's first outing in his backyard taught him that even a sleeping bag rated to plus-20 degrees offered slim protection against a cold, early winter evening. But while he was breathing the polar air inside his pup tent, God breathed into Bob a powerful vision, challenging him to "the fellowship of sharing in his sufferings" (Philippians 3:10, NIV). God weeps when His people suffer, so He was inviting Bob to weep with Him for the poor of Wayzata, Minnesota.

In November 1996, Bob committed to sleeping out in his tent until he raised $7,000 to buy Thanksgiving dinners for 100 families. In fourteen days, Bob was back in his warm bed with $10,000 collected for meals. But his journey of obedience in response to God's invitation had just begun. A local ministry, Interfaith Outreach and Community Partners, challenged Bob to sleep out again the next year for the working poor and homeless. Thus was born Bob's Sleep Out. It quickly morphed from one cobbler's mission to a community-wide commitment to the Samaritan women of this largely affluent suburb of Minneapolis. Since 1996, thousands of community members, including churches, businesses, and youth and civic groups have raised millions of dollars to provide shelter for the homeless.

One of my favorite photos of our son Josh was taken when he supported Bob's Sleep Out his junior year in high school. Bob showed up at midnight, in driving rain in the middle of a goose-poop-infested football field, to encourage Josh and all of his classmates as they lived their faith out loud. The picture shows Bob with fifty wide-eyed, wet, and freezing-cold high school students hanging on his every word. For them, he was "Jesus with skin on" that evening in front of their tents. If he were merely preaching a sermon, they would have crawled back into the relative warmth of their sleeping bags. But a sermon lived out in self-less actions was worthy of time spent standing out in the cold and rain.

Do not let Bob's story intimidate you into inaction. Many acts of generosity are a smaller response to the most basic needs of the poor and hungry. The cumulative effect of thousands of small, individual actions have the power to make a vast difference.

Zippers for Jesus

Several years ago I was running out of the office, late as usual, to catch a flight. "Do you want any money?"our office manager Susan asked, as I sprinted past her desk. "Who doesn't?" I thought.

It turned out that we had sold a large number of books at a conference the evening before, and Susan was sitting on a pile of cash. She was offering to unload some of it on me rather than take it all to the bank. Impulsively I replied, "I'll take all you've got!" I stuffed $750 in small bills into my roll aboard and scrambled off to the airport. Only when I was walking through the scanners at the terminal did it occur to me that I looked like a drug runner!

I had the wild idea of giving the money away to participants in a *STEWARDshift*™ program that I was facilitating the next day in Seattle. That evening, I sat on the bed in my hotel room and sorted the money into 100 envelopes, each containing between $2 and $60. The following day, I challenged each participant to follow a certain rhythm with the money and see how God responded as a result. God blesses each of us. Some get a little; some get much more. Regardless of what they received, each participant was to *pray* for God's guidance, *give* the money away, *watch* where it went, and, if they were willing, *share* the outcome of their generosity. The only nonnegotiable was that they had to give it all away. They could not keep the cash. The task was simply to follow God's Isaiah 58 directive—in other words, to take God at His word. This was honestly the best idea I had all year!

One of the recipients of the envelopes was Pastor Jack. He in turn added some of his own money, subdivided it into twelve new envelopes, and passed them along with the same instructions to his confirmation class: *pray, give, watch,* and *share.* Several weeks later, he sent their initial reactions via e-mail:

> *The group was far more quiet and serious than usual. I outlined the pray-give-watch-share plan with them. We paused in quiet prayer . . . asking for discernment on*

how to be a faithful conduit of whatever was in the envelope. Then, as each opened theirs, no one was disappointed or giddy as I really think the prayer beforehand made them realize this was theirs to give— not keep. One of the rougher, but lovable guys told the others, "Remember, God and Pastor Jack will be pissed if we pocket it for ourselves!" Success!!

What did these empowered ninth graders do with the money in order to not "piss off" God or Pastor Jack? Two guys pooled their $27, bought ten pounds of sliced turkey and ham, a jar of peanut butter, some jelly, and loaves of bread, and made "a mess of sandwiches" for the Gospel Mission's Men's and Women's Shelters. I'm assuming they didn't make peanut butter and ham sandwiches.

One girl used her $5 for a new zipper to repair an unused coat and donated it to a local clothing drive. Another girl bought $11 worth of Taco Bell certificates to hand out to the frequent panhandlers on the interstate exit ramps. Three others went to make toy purchases for the Marines Toys for Tots drive. Each of these cool ninth-graders heard the call of the poor for basic needs and answered with simple, but profound creativity and compassion.

Giving *and* Getting

God promises to reward such generosity with a series of powerful outcomes in Isaiah 58:

Do this and the lights will turn on, and your lives will turn around at once. Your righteousness will pave your way. The God of glory will secure your passage. Then when you pray, God will answer. You'll call out for help and I'll say, "Here I am." I will always show you where to go. I'll give you a full life in the emptiest of places—firm muscles, strong bones. You'll be like a well-watered garden, a gurgling spring that never runs dry (verses 8-9, 11).

If we want to hear God's voice, we need only hear the poor. If we want to be spiritually well hydrated, we must attend to the parched interstate panhandlers. If we want the lights to stay on in our house, we need to keep the lights on for the homeless. If we want to draw closer to God, we need to pull up next to the poor.

God does not mandate a tithe of time or money in the New Testament. He is not into grudge giving—where we feel forced to give—or greed giving—where we give in order to get. He simply desires that we move from *serve-us* religion to authentic service in the name of Jesus.

The gift He requires from us is for us "to act justly, to love mercy and to walk humbly" (Micah 6:8, NIV), especially with people on the margins. Rather than pervert the gospel into a cheesy "give to get scheme," Jesus reveals the outcome of true godly generosity in His unlikely interaction with the Samaritan woman. She gave what she had—all that she had—and lives were changed forever.

As a result of His inquiry and her response to give what she had, the woman runs to her village and brings all of her judgmental townies out to meet Jesus. The poor Samaritan woman becomes a powerful missionary, igniting a revival in a long-scorned land. Jesus stays on two more days with the Samaritans at their invitation, harvesting the rewards of the once-lonely woman's gift of water for a weary rabbi.

Just as with the Samaritan woman, Jesus asks us for *our* help today. Through our actions, the poor are fed, the naked clothed, and the prisoners set free. What do we get in return? We are freed from our own slavery to selfishness and can fully experience the pure joy of a ninth-grader's gift of a zippered coat. Jesus offers us living water that does not run dry and spiritual food that never ceases to satisfy. Through our generosity, we become like a well-watered garden to which others are drawn for nourishment and survival.

To give is more blessed than to receive. Actually, it is *only* in giving that we truly receive the best stuff! Jesus seeks to check our level of commitment to others and to Him with His last, most important question, *"Do you truly love Me?"*

REFLECT AND RESPOND

READ the following Scriptures:
- Isaiah 58:1-14
- Philippians 3:8-10

REFLECT on the following questions:
1. Rather than bearing the suffering that cries out in the world today, what current world events are breaking your heart because they are breaking the heart of God?
2. What is your answer to *Time* magazine's cover story question, "Does God Want You to be Rich?"
3. Which of the promises in Isaiah 58:8-14 do you find most exhilarating?

RESPOND to the following challenge:
- Take the same *Pray-Give-Watch-Share* challenge as Pastor Jack's kids with a small group of your friends over the next thirty days, and see where and how God blesses your efforts.
- You aren't done until you share with others what has happened. Who will you share with? Set a meeting time.

When they had finished eating, Jesus said to Simon Peter,
"Simon son of John, do you truly love me more than
these?" "Yes Lord," he said, "you know that I love you."
Jesus said, "Feed my Lambs." Again Jesus said, "Simon
son of John, do you truly love me?" He answered,
"Yes, Lord, you know that I love you." Jesus said,
"Take care of my sheep." The third time he said to him,
"Simon son of John, do you love me?" Peter was hurt
because Jesus asked him the third time, "Do you love me?"
He said, "Lord, you know all things; you know
that I love you." Jesus said, "Feed my sheep."

—

John 21:15-17, NIV

Chapter Eight

DO YOU TRULY LOVE ME?

THE QUESTION OF LOVE

Where's the Big Guy?

My friend Keith is a study in physical and personality contrasts, much of it based on what he did for a living for many years.

On the one hand, he is a mountain of a man, standing 6' 7" tall with striking features and huge, gnarled hands. At the same time, his imposing body is breaking down bit-by-bit, the result of fourteen years spent in the trenches of professional football. Keith anchored the offensive line in two

Super Bowl victories and faced the violent rush of defensive linemen bent on sacking Joe Montana.

You don't spend fourteen years in the NFL without a tough, competitive, sometimes-brutal attitude. Yet Keith's spirit is as soft and transparent as any man I know. His heart melts at the requests of his wife and three daughters. He stood in an exhilarating arena where so many boys—and yes, even men—dream of playing yet speaks of those days only when asked. Keith is a humble warrior. For all of these reasons and many more, he has become one of my dearest friends over the past twenty years.

One Friday more than a decade ago, Keith revealed to our Friday guy's group that he was dying. We sat in stunned silence. He told us that he had suffered from polycystic kidney disease all of his life. Now, his tumor-choked kidneys were shutting down. Keith had submitted his name for organ donation, but the wait to receive a cadaver kidney averaged more than four years. He—and his doctor—feared that he did not have that long to live. His next step to survive was dialysis, but he was trying to avoid that painful daily routine to preserve the integrity of his kidneys. His condition was deteriorating rapidly.

"Coincidentally," on this same Friday, Apham was visiting our group for the first time. He had been invited by one of our regular attendees to describe his passion for starting a Christian radio station in his native country of Nigeria. He happened to be there the morning Keith described his failing health.

Apham told us later that he felt the kind of natural compassion for Keith you would expect to have when someone shares that they are dying. But he really didn't feel any deep emotional connection to him. He didn't know Keith. And truth be told, the one single time he had given any serious thought to the topic of organ donation was just a few years earlier. He wasn't sure why he felt so strongly about it, but when his wife Janel told him she had check marked the box on her driver's license renewal form, indicating she would donate her organs in the event of death, Apham had passionately argued that she needed to go back and opt out of the program. Apham was a good man, a godly man, a compassionate man, but donating one's organs held a certain revulsion for him that erupted to the surface when Janel told him what she had done. He let her know that it was his strong opinion that if she passed away in some tragic accident, "she would be going to meet God with all of her organs intact!"

Apham shared with our group his basic plan to minister in Nigeria and asked for our support. He would be leaving for the place of his birth in the next few weeks for an exploratory trip to assess the opportunities, obstacles, and true viability of starting a Christian radio station. We asked him to report back on his return to help us know how we could support him spiritually and possibly financially.

While in Nigeria, he was reminded over and over of the crushing conditions and staggering needs of this country. One of the most poignant moments for him was a street encounter with a woman hoping to generate pity by using her dying child as a prop to help her beg for food. She and her child's suffering—on so many levels—were almost overwhelming to his spirit. But it was in that moment God spoke to him of another person in need, someone he hadn't thought of in weeks. Beginning in that moment, no matter how hard he tried, Apham could not push the memory of Keith's condition from his mind. God kept snapping Keith back into Apham's heart's focus through the lives and circumstances he encountered daily in Nigeria.

Apham followed his heart's desire to create a ministry in Nigeria. But that was not all that God was leading him to do.

When Apham returned to our group several weeks later, his first question was, "Where's the big guy?" Keith was absent. We gave Apham the sobering update. Most nights Keith would lie shivering in bed, unable to get warm, even when wrapped in a down coat and comforter. He knew he was dying, but his deterioration was accelerating much faster than anticipated.

That day, Apham became the fifth man in our group of twelve to inquire about donating a kidney to Keith.

Miracles Never Cease

What makes Apham's offer so remarkable was that he had only met Keith one time—the morning Keith told our group he was dying—and his first, gut-level and honest reaction was not favorable toward donating an organ.

The story moves from remarkable to miraculous when you consider that Apham, a life-long Oakland Raiders fan, was offering to donate his kidney to Keith, who played his entire career for the archrival San Francisco 49ers. God's love really does conquer all and miracles never cease!

Okay, you know that I am being lighthearted about a sports rivalry needing a divine touch to overcome, but you might be one of those diehard fans who agrees!

Fast-forward to a cold, overcast, gloomy Sunday in February two months later. After slogging two blocks through the snow and sleet from our parked car, Carol and I ran into Apham and his family as we entered church. His answer to my benign query, "What's up?" was stunning.

"Well," he said with a smile, "I lost my job, and this week

I donate one of my kidneys to Keith!" What are the chances that a Nigerian man, in the U.S. for only ten years, would be a *perfect match* for a native Minnesotan, fifteen years his elder, from the small town of St. Cloud? The only thing that they had in common was a shared passion for American football—and their faith. That qualifies as a "God thing"! Only God could have been orchestrating this miraculous connection decades in advance.

But Apham still had to say "Yes," in response to God's question, "Do you truly love Me?" He needed to pay attention to all of the people and markers God was putting in his path.

The Death of a Dream

Jesus confronted Peter, His most charismatic and impulsive follower, with a piercing question of love shortly after His resurrection. Jesus' closest followers had returned almost immediately to their former profession in the days following His death. Just three years earlier, Jesus had challenged them to put down their nets and take up His calling to become fishers of men (Matthew 4:19). But now, having watched their leader suffer a brutal and inglorious death, they were wondering if they had just spent the previous three years betting on the wrong horse.

The king was dead and their Camelot appeared to be nothing more than a mist, so real one day but evaporating before their very eyes. This was the death of a dream.

Many of us have experienced the crushing defeat of disillusionment. Respected pastors of influential churches have been exposed as frequent practitioners of the very moral failure they condemn every Sunday morning. Business leaders have traded away whole companies of multigenerational employees in the name of progress and innovation. A child was lost in an accident. The love of one's life left for another person.

But the followers of Jesus had the added burden of believing that He was the Promised One. They had staked their whole life and livelihood on following Jesus not as *a* Messiah but as *the* Messiah. Not only had they lost a friend and leader; they had lost their faith.

Only days earlier, Peter had pledged his allegiance to Jesus—"Master, I'm ready for anything with you. I'd go to jail for you. I'd die for you!" (Luke 22:33). This was Peter's style. Boldness and bombast. Peter is not like John, who "leaned back against Jesus" (John 21:20, NIV). Peter was a talk-first-think-later guy. He lived his adoration of Jesus fully out loud. Peter is the patron saint of all ADHD Jesus-followers!

Shortly after his bold claim, however, Peter denied even

knowing Jesus to save his own skin. Now, with hopes dashed and only the bitter memory of recent failure, Peter was sitting in his skivvies in the middle of the lake soaking worms. Adding insult to injury, it appeared that the three-year layoff from fishing had diminished his skill. He had spent the whole evening with friends getting totally skunked!

Never forget, no matter how dark and confusing the situation you face, Jesus is always near. Jesus enters into Peter's gloom, demonstrating for all time that He has real power over death and evil. He shows up not as some ethereal vapor but as a real person, cooking over a campfire. Jesus serves up a shore breakfast to a small cadre of discouraged, disheartened, and disillusioned men, proving once again that He is attentive not only to our spiritual needs but also to our most basic physical requirements. It is at this inaugural prayer breakfast that He asks Peter what appears to be the same question three different times.

Jesus is not assuming that Peter or we are slow of head or hard of heart. He is asking three distinct questions, all aimed at clarifying the intensity of our love for Him. Do we truly love Him, *more than these* other things that would dim our devotion? Do *we* truly love Him, enough to ultimately trust His desires for us? Do we *love* Him, not like casual acquaintances but with unrestrained passion and purpose?

Each of these questions goes to the very core of our deepening faith journey. Our answers define the focus of our faith and the enjoyment of our existence. Jesus asks, but we must answer His penetrating three-fold question of love.

Pushing the Reset Button

I experience the famous line from the movie *The Sixth Sense* almost every time I step into a crowded elevator in an office building or corporate headquarters: "I see dead people." People are numbed from the heart up by the incessant musak of memos and busy-ness of business. The illusion of technology as the ticket to a more leisurely life has given way to the reality of a 24/7 world of connectivity. A friend recently made an observation I am having a hard time discounting: "technology is the new idolatry." He was basing this on watching a person go forward in church to receive Holy Communion, head bowed not in prayer, but feverishly working his smart phone. The pretense that because we are *so* important, we must remain tethered at all times, and at any cost to our office, colleagues, and friends, is choking our human spirit. We know intuitively that having more is not a promise of peace but a near or full addiction that will ultimately demand our health, relationships, faith, even our life as payment. Yet we press on, surreptitiously doing the iPrayer whenever and wherever we can sneak it in—even Communion.

Our harried, hurry sickness has given way to pandemic illness. Years of stuffing down "cup-holder cuisine" have resulted in bloated bodies and significance-starved souls.

Jesus sweeps His hand over this whole scene and asks, "Do you truly love Me *more than these*?" What is Jesus really asking of Peter and us? Perhaps He was referring to the large haul of fish and is questioning whether we are prepared to loosen our dependence on all of our false securities, including work, in order to fully grasp a total reliance on Him. Undoubtedly Jesus was calling out Peter and his buddies for their rapid retreat to the comforts of their former job.

Apham was laid off right before his kidney donation, freeing him to answer God's question posed through Keith with a resounding "Yes!" The invalid by the pool set down his vocation of begging in order to pick up his calling to heal others. The Samaritan woman at the well put aside her daily work of fetching water in order to gather up followers of Jesus. What must we let go of?

Jesus asks us if we love Him more than the rush of life in order to place our priorities in perspective. When placed in the queue behind our devotion to God, everything finds new and deeper purpose and meaning. Even our service to God needs to step into line. Dallas Willard suggests, "The greatest enemy of intimacy *with* God is service *to* God." It seems paradoxical, but for most of us the biggest spiritual danger we face is not in the temptation to commit gross sins. It is busy-ness, even—and especially—for God's sake.

Just As We Were?

I was always moved by the throng of people stepping forward at the conclusion of every Billy Graham Crusade. They came from the upper decks and bleacher seats, responding to the message, and moving with the stanzas of the old hymn, "Just as I Am." Far too often we sing "Just As I Am," and we come *just as we are,* but we live *just as we were.* We are being challenged in Jesus' question to reprioritize our lives in favor of never again living *just as we were.* Peter's response to Jesus' question was, "You are my Master, and You know I love you more than I love these stinky fish." How do I know he said the part about stinky fish? Peter put down, once and forever, fishing for mere fish.

Is He more important than our busy-ness? Would our response to Jesus' question be the same as Peter's? What needs to step to the back of our to-do list in order for us to leap boldly into uncharted territory to become a fully devoted follower of Jesus like Peter?

Met by Jeff at the Pearly Gates

One of the verses in the Bible that speaks to me most powerfully about God's redemptive and restorative love is Mark 16:7. An angel tells three women who sought to anoint Jesus' dead body in the grave to run and get His followers together for a joyous reunion. There are two words I don't want you to miss. "But go, tell his disciples *and Peter*, 'He is going ahead of you into Galilee. There you will see him, just as he told you'" (NIV, italics added).

You didn't miss them did you?

And Peter. Those two little words say it all. Jesus wanted specifically and especially to reconnect with Peter after his three-fold denial in the courtyard. He wanted to reassure Peter that no one has sinned so greatly as to disqualify them from God's grace.

How do you picture heaven? Do you envision it like the beginning of many old and tired jokes, "So a guy dies and goes to heaven. There, he's met at the pearly gates by St. Peter, and—" Do you see an old guy with white hair, a white robe, and a halo over his head, waiting to ask you a few test questions before he checks you in?

My grandfather wrote a beautiful little book on heaven, inspired in part by his experience of ministering to Lester Kahl, a convicted murderer, just before Lester was hanged. I am sure he was thinking of reuniting with Lester at the pearly gates as he wrote.

In your picture of heaven, do you ever imagine being met at the pearly gates by Jeffrey Dahmer? Dahmer's name and image is synonymous with "monster." Between 1978 and 1991, he raped, murdered, and dismembered seventeen young boys and men. He ate at least one corpse. He stored his victims in vats. As punishment for his heinous crimes, the court imposed fifteen consecutive life sentences, thus requiring that Jeffrey Dahmer serve a minimum of 936 years in prison. On November 28, 1994, a fellow inmate killed Dahmer with a single blow to the skull. It would seem that this sickest of stories ended in the Columbia Correctional Institution in Portage, Wisconsin.

But Peter's story did not end with his denials, and Jeffrey Dahmer's story did not end with his incarceration. Six months before his death, Dahmer was baptized by immersion in a whirlpool tub by Roy Ratcliff, a local minister. After his conversion, Dahmer began meeting on a weekly basis to pray and study Scripture. Perhaps now he joins the ranks of other murderers in heaven such as the apostle Paul, Moses, and King David. If so, I would say he is keeping pretty good company.

Is your view of God's redemptive and restorative grace

deep and wide enough to greet Jeff at the gates of heaven? If you're like me, such a scenario causes me to pull up and think.

The Net Won't Break

Before Jesus fed Peter and his companions breakfast, before He asked Peter if he truly loved Him, Jesus helped Peter bring in an incredible haul of fish on his last fishing expedition.

Jesus spoke to them: "Good morning! Did you catch anything for breakfast?" They answered, "No." He said, "Throw the net off the right side of the boat and see what happens." They did what he said. All of a sudden there were so many fish in it, they weren't strong enough to pull it in (John 21:5-6).

When Peter realizes it is Jesus on the shore, he dives into the water to swim to meet Him. He's so excited to see Jesus that he makes his colleagues bring the boat to land. But his friends don't let him off the hook that easily—they make him tug the net up on shore. It is in this part of the story that John shares two fascinating little tidbits: "Jesus said, 'Bring some of the fish you've just caught.' Simon Peter joined them and pulled the net to shore—153 big fish! And even with all those fish, the net didn't rip" (verses 10-11).

There weren't 154 or 152 fish in the haul. There were exactly 153. Why does that number matter? And do we really care that the net didn't rip? It might have sounded more impressive if the net did rip.

The fourth-century biblical scholar Jerome offers an explanation for the specificity of John's account.

In the sea, there are 153 different kinds of fish: and that the catch is one which includes every kind of fish: and that therefore the number symbolizes the fact that someday all people of all nations will be gathered together in Christ. This great catch of fishes was gathered into the net, and the net held them all and was not broken. The net stands for the church: and there is room in the church for all people of all nations.

There is even room in the church for Peter and for us—and for Jeffrey Dahmer.

The grace that holds the church together is strong enough that not even Peter or us or Jeffrey can break its chords of love.

In asking the question, "Do *you* truly love Me?" Jesus is checking whether we really believe that all people are so precious in His sight that we are willing to put down our prejudices, preconceptions, and hatreds.

But Do *You?*

Jesus asks Peter, "Do *you* truly love Me?" He does not ask, "Do you think John loves Me? What about James? And Thomas—that dude sure has some doubts! As a matter of fact, I think from now on I will label him 'doubting Thomas'!"

No, Jesus asks Peter for *his* personal commitment. He desires the same from each of us. Do *I* truly love Him? Do you truly love Him?

In a 2008 research project I learned the percentage of Americans who have never known:

- a Buddhist–59 percent
- an undocumented immigrant–54 percent
- a Muslim–46 percent
- a homeless person–45 percent
- an evangelical Christian–40 percent
- a political liberal–25 percent
- a political conservative–24 percent
- a former inmate–15 percent
- a wealthy person–12 percent

Given our ignorance of others, we had better speak only for ourselves. Jesus asks, "Do you truly love Me?" Do we trust that the net will not break, no matter the size and scope of His catch? No matter who comes into His kingdom? Can we lay aside believing that we know which varieties of fish are considered a "good catch"?

Unconditional Love

Words matter. *Love* has many profound and deep meanings in the English language, but overall it has been cheapened by tawdry TV shows and Hollywood portrayals of uncommitted, bed-hopping sex. Our familiarity with the word *love* diminishes its significance, and our casual misuse of it distorts its power.

But love is at the heart of our understanding of God's great narrative played out across the span of Scripture. Love appears over 750 times in the Bible. It is the core of His mission. Love is the center of God's two great commands to us—to love God and to love our neighbor. (See Matthew 22:36-38.) There are many wonderful attributes that we can possess, but according to Paul, "the greatest of these is love" (1 Corinthians 13:13, NIV). He also says:

"No matter what I say, what I believe, and what I do, I'm bankrupt without love" (1 Corinthians 13:3).

So when Jesus asks Peter, "Do you love Me?" He is getting to the core of the most important dynamic of faith for him and for us.

189

John tells us that Peter was hurt because Jesus asked him a third time if he loved Him (21:17).

Didn't you hear me the first two times?

Actually, Peter was not hurt by the recurrence of the question. In fact, he was likely relieved by Jesus' grace in asking three times in exchange for Peter's three denials.

To understand what hurt him, we must understand the wordplay happening between him and Jesus.

The first time Jesus asks Peter if he loves Him, He uses the strong Greek word *agape*, which is a selfless, sacrificial, unconditional love for others.

In Peter's response, "Yes, Lord, You know that I love You," he substitutes the Greek word *phileo*—a deep friendship—for the Greek word Jesus used, *agape,* which defines the unconditional love of God.

It would be like asking the love of your life, "Do you love me with all your heart?" and hear them answer, "Of course, I like you a lot."

Again in verse 16, Jesus asks Peter, "Do you love me?" using the word *agape*. Peter responds a second time, "Yes, Master, you know that I love [*phileo*] you." I like you a lot. You're my buddy. You might even be my BFF.

What happens next is fascinating. Jesus asks the seminal question a third time, but now He uses the weaker word *phileo* instead of *agape.* In essence, He is asking Peter and us, "Do you just want to be my buddy, my pal, my friend—or are you totally sold out; do you love Me with an abandoned, unconditional, wholehearted love, regardless of the consequences or price-tag?" Is your love for Me *agape,* or is it *phileo*?

Of all the questions we've walked through in *Dare to Answer*, this is *the* question. Are we willing to abandon our busy-ness and the false security that inhibits our intimacy with the Almighty? Are we able to set aside our prejudice and the narcissism of small differences that prevents us from loving our neighbors as ourselves? Are we prepared to move from a deep friendship or even a familial love to total devotion to our Creator? Are we sold out to Jesus?

As soon as Peter grasped what Jesus was asking, he was hurt. His faith and devotion were being called into question. Peter became more reflective and careful with his word choice. He answered this time: "Master, you know everything there is to know. You've got to know that I love you" (21:17).

I find it profound—and I believe it is a result of this encounter—that Peter never again used the weaker word *phileo* in any of his recorded speaking or writings.

As we read on in John 21, Jesus accepts and affirms Peter's profession of love. He lets Peter know that even under persecution, He is confident that Peter will be as strong as his name.

And Peter was. He was crucified upside down for boldly proclaiming and practicing the *agape* love of Jesus.

Jesus' last command to Peter and to us is to follow Him. Following Jesus. This takes us back to the first question of the book: What do you want? When what we want is to follow Jesus, our lives are never the same. It is what empowered the disciples of John the Baptist to "come and see" and the fearless followers of Jesus to "go and be."

Are we ready to follow? We must first answer for ourselves Jesus' questions of our desire, fear, wholeness, identity, forgiveness, wealth, generosity, and love. Only then are we prepared to enter into and practice the deep faith to which He calls us.

One Glorious Day

One glorious day it will be thrilling to meet John's disciples, the fearful lake-crossers, the beggar of Bethesda, the liberated grave-dweller, the town whore, many of the well-fed crowd of 5,000, Peter, Lester, Jeffrey, and each other in heaven. It promises to be exhilarating. I look forward to meeting you there as well. We'll have eternity to get to know these wonderful people who experienced God's grace—and each other. Until then, may God richly bless you as you continue to live in His questions and draw ever closer to Him.

REFLECT AND RESPOND

READ the following Scripture:
- 1 Corinthians 13:1-13
- Matthew 22:34-40

REFLECT on the following questions:

1. Does your service *to* God get in the way of your intimacy *with* God?

2. How do you picture heaven? Who do you most look forward to meeting? With whom do you most look forward to reuniting? Who would you be most surprised to see?

3. Do you express *agape* or *phileo* love for God?

RESPOND to the following challenge:

- Assess your time commitments. Do any of your priorities—work, relationships, health, finances—need to be reprioritized so that they do not diminish your devotion to God?

- Don't stop with assessment. Sit down with your calendar of activities and appointments and actively work on reprioritizing your schedule over the next thirty days.

A WORD AFTER

I began by observing that Jesus asked some questions that require brave answers. Those answers, especially when they reflect our deepest heart, take time. In looking at men and women considered to have lived an honest and examined faith—Mother Teresa, Pope Francis, Albert Schweitzer, Dietrich Bonhoeffer—one quickly notices that they are all old. I am not saying that you cannot answer hard questions and be young at the same time. But deep thoughts, love, wisdom, and friendship are often formed over many years and even accompanied by scar tissue.

David Brooks recently observed at the Aspen Ideas Festival, "The things that lead you astray, those things are fast—lust, fear, vanity, gluttony. The things we admire most—honesty, humility, self-control, courage—those things take time and they accumulate slowly."

If you are more restless than relieved by Jesus' questions, take heart. All of His provocative questions are intended to draw us closer to and deepen our faith in Him. But discerning God's desire for our life, overcoming our own fear, seeking wholeness, claiming our identity as a Jesus-follower, extending genuine forgiveness, understanding true wealth, practicing real generosity, and whole-heartedly loving God— these all take time and patience.

I'm challenged daily by each question, and I bet you are too. Truly living a deep faith is a life-long pursuit. Here's my encouragement: Make it all a matter of daily prayer. Not just any prayer though. Take a shot at living the prayer penned by Brennan Manning:

"I surrender my will and my life to you today, without reservation and with humble confidence for you are my loving Father.

Set me free from self-consciousness, from anxiety about yesterday and tomorrow and from the tyranny of the approval and disapproval of others, that I may find joy and delight simply and solely in pleasing you.

Let your plan for my life and the lives of all your children gracefully unfold one day at a time."

Slow down. Be graceful with yourself. Live into the questions without having to know all of the answers. Enjoy the wild ride of a deepening faith that is drawing you closer to the One who risked everything to call you His friend.

—JB

About the Author

John Busacker is a writer, speaker, and entrepreneur. He is the author of four books—including *do less, be more: The Life-Changing Power of Focus* (Worthy). John is a sought-after keynote speaker, engaging such issues as personal focus, leadership character, holistic generosity, and winsome faith in the marketplace. He is the Founder of *Life*-Worth, LLC, and is a member of the Duke Corporate Education Global Learning Resource Network. John enjoys running, cycling, and spending time supporting the development needs of leaders with a variety of faith-based organizations in the U.S. and sub-Saharan Africa. John and his wife Carol live in Excelsior, Minnesota, and have two adult sons, a delightful daughter-in-law, and a perfect granddaughter.

jbusacker@johnbusacker.com

WORTHY®
Inspired

If you enjoyed this book, will you consider sharing
the message with others?

- Mention the book in a Facebook post, Twitter update, Pinterest pin, blog post, or upload a picture through Instagram.
- Recommend this book to those in your small group, book club, workplace, and classes.
- Head over to facebook.com/worthypublishing, "LIKE" the page, and post a comment as to what you enjoyed the most.
- Pick up a copy for someone you know who would be challenged and encouraged by this message.
- Write a book review online.

You can subscribe to Worthy Publishing's
newsletter at worthypublishing.com.

Worthy Publishing Facebook Page   Worthy Publishing Website